Praying the Price

Stuart Robinson

Sovereign World

Sovereign World Ltd
PO Box 777
Tonbridge
Kent TN11 0ZS
England

ISBN: 1 85240 152 4

This Sovereign World book is distributed in North America by
Renew Books, a ministry of Gospel Light, Ventura, California,
USA. For a free catalog of resources from Renew Books/
Gospel Light, please contact your Christian supplier or call
1-800-4-GOSPEL.

Typeset by CRB Associates, Drayton, Norwich.
Printed in England by Clays Ltd, St Ives plc.

Author's Note

After studying many churches in Great Britain, Roy Pointer concluded that corporate and personal prayer is an essential 'sign of growth found in every growing church. The church that never prays does not grow.'[1]

Remarkable church growth has been happening for some time in Korea, China and Argentina. In each case prayer is claimed to be a decisive factor.

However in the West, at least in books on church growth, prayer hardly rates more than footnote status. In our programming it is accorded nodding necessity.

This book addresses this strange omission.

Although it is difficult, if not impossible, to be dogmatic in matters where the supernatural and natural interact, nevertheless there is sufficient evidence, biblical, historical and contemporary to highlight a major factor – a relationship between prayer and growth in the church, which if overlooked only increases the probability of continued decline of the church in western society.

This book is not just a survey of biblical, historical and contemporary data. It proceeds to outline clearly the steps that need to be taken so that prayer may become a central factor in the growth and life of any church.

1. Pointer, Roy. *Ten Signs of Church Growth*. (Chapter reprinted in *New Life*, Melbourne, June 18, 1987.)

To Margaret
Krystal, Kynan and Kiron
Family
Co-workers
Caring Companions

Contents

Contents

Foreword

The book you have in your hands is as one of the first bright rays of light when the sun comes over the horizon to signal a new day!

The new day is the beginning of the intentional, aggressive application of effective prayer to the growth of the church. True, throughout the decades an implicit acknowledgment of prayer as a fundamental base for not only growth but for the total life of the church in general has been common. But *Praying the Price* is different. The implicit has now become refreshingly explicit. Stuart Robinson has shown us not only how prayer *should* relate to church growth, but more importantly how it actually *does* relate to church growth and how it *can* relate even more directly.

Understandably, God would have chosen a very special person to write a pioneer book such as this one. The author would need to be an individual personally consumed by prayer and fired by the need to challenge others to move more strongly into effective prayer. Equally important, is that the author be a practising pastor, day in and day out, in personal contact with all the joys and all the pains of real people in real churches. But not any praying pastor could do this well. The author also needs to have professional expertise on theories of church growth which enable one to analyze accurately what one observes. Finally, for the book to be useful, the author would need to be a good communicator.

No wonder God chose Stuart Robinson for the task. Stuart brings all the above qualities and more to give us this sustained, thoroughly researched treatise on how prayer relates to virtually every principal aspect of church life.

Stuart does not write in a vacuum. I am impressed with the way he makes ample reference to most of the key players in the great worldwide prayer movement of today. The prayer movement has been building momentum over two decades, and Stuart Robinson provides exciting information as to its progress. Because Stuart has been such an avid learner, God has allowed him to be an inspiring teacher.

The prayer movement has been developing impressive networks of communication between its multitudinous segments, and I hope *Praying the Price* finds its way through all of them into the hands of every pastor and prayer leader of the nations. If it does, the rays of the rising sun will surely burst forth with the full light of this new day in God's kingdom.

C. Peter Wagner
Fuller Theological Seminary
Pasadena, California

Introduction

In 1952, Albert Einstein was asked by a Princeton doctoral student what was left in the world for original dissertation research. Einstein's reply was, 'Find out about prayer.'[1]

What a challenge! Whether or not the student followed the advice is unrecorded. Certainly the options for definitive conclusions are few, for 'prayer in the divine economy is a fantastically puzzling mystery.'[2]

Within the Bible there are many encouragements, invitations, urgings and even commands to pray, but there is never given any explanation of just how the process works. That it does is amply testified to in biblical and Christian history, but how it does so remains beyond honest comprehension. Human inquisitiveness is usually tantalised by fascination with the unknown and is prompted to probe or speculate further to remove all mystery. Perhaps for this reason books on prayer continue to be written and sell steadily. Yet our ability to investigate is often not matched by our willingness to practise.

Such is often the lament of missionary strategists. For example:

> 'Prayer meetings in most churches are poorly attended, and missionary prayer meetings are usually left to the elderly. Can it be that we have tried to analyse and categorise prayer into a manageable science and then

11

turned away in despair when it defies our attempts to contain it?'[3]

'Prayerlessness is the church's major malady.'[4]

'There are progressive dinners, visits to old people's homes, youth outings, musician's practices, home Bible studies and numerous committees. But where have all the prayer meetings gone?'[5]

While the above leaders of the Overseas Missionary Fellowship, SIM International, and World Evangelisation Crusade respectively, highlighted the need, missiologist George Peters a decade earlier had spelt out the challenge when he said, 'reaching the unreached will, first of all, mean for us not only to lay hold ... in faith, but to develop thousands upon thousands of prayer cells.'[6]

Others readily concur that the greatest lack in the church today is neither people nor funds. 'The greatest need is prayer. Without increasing the number of Christian workers or their financial support, we could see multiplied results if we would only multiply prayer.'[7]

Since the 1970s interest has been steadily rekindled. Bob Willhite considers that interest in prayer has never before been greater 'in this age.'[8]

Dick Eastman points out that we are today blessed with scores of godly authors[9] on the subject, and then goes on to list what he considers to be, for him, seventy-five of the most influential.[10] In very recent years C. Peter Wagner has done much both to document and nurture this new interest, which he refers to now as a 'great prayer movement'[11] which began in 1970. He predicts that the movement, born in the seventies, will blossom 'in the 1990s with a quantity and an intensity ... that we have never seen before.'[12]

From Eastern Europe, Peter Kuzmic reports massive changes on the political and religious scenes in the former Soviet Union, Poland, Czechoslovakia, Hungary, Romania, Bulgaria, Albania, and what was previously Yugoslavia.[13] He is reported as saying that in some of these cases 'the single most important reason for growth' in the churches is concerted prayer. [14] Similarly, David Bryant reports on prayer movements in the Philippines, France, the Middle East, Japan, Switzerland, China, New Zealand, Brazil, Argentina, and South Africa. [15]

In Australia, the Evangelical Alliance is but one nation-wide organisation which has called for extraordinary prayer. In 1989 and 1990, they challenged churches to set aside one hundred days for a continuous 'canopy of prayer' over Australia. The Australian Fellowship of Church Growth gave an entire bulletin over to the subject. [16]

Harold Lindsell is but one of many today who believes that prayer is 'the greatest of all weapons' which the church possesses. Because of this he claims the church 'has more fire power than all the armies of the world put together.' He then goes on to cite twenty-seven outstanding examples in history where prayer was the factor in altering the lives of individuals and nations. [17]

Regarding prayer, the need has been highlighted, the challenge has been issued, and its effectiveness is acknowledged. So what is resulting in harnessing 'the movement' and riding on a new wave of hoped-for church growth? The answer may be 'not much' – at least in the western world. While there is an increasing amount of popular literature and not a little noise from pulpits, perhaps 'each man stands convicted at the bar of his own conscience' [18] regarding the church's appearance of relative prayerlessness.

It is acknowledged that 'the quantitative, qualitative, and organic increase in a local body of believers is a supernatural process.' [19] We have a part to play. However, only God can make it grow (1 Corinthians 3:6). The access we have to him is through prayer. Yet only occasionally do local pastors seem to identify and practise a linkage between prayer and growth in their churches.

English preacher, Sidlow Baxter, is one such. He says:

'I have pastored only three churches in my more than sixty years of ministry. We had revival in every one.

And not one of them came as a result of my preaching. They came as a result of membership entering into a covenant to pray until revival came. And it did come, every time.' [20]

Mike Johnson of Calvary Temple, Assembly of God, Springfield, Illinois, also saw his church grow from zero to 2,100 in nine years. [21] Johnson, in explaining this phenomenon says, 'The first key to church growth is prayer.' [22] Of the other pastors in his denomination, 121 concurred. In a survey among them they ranked prayer as the primary factor in church growth. [23]

The paradox is that while there is a grass roots movement emerging, both talking about and practising prayer and seeing resultant growth in some churches, the more serious writers, theorists and researchers of the church growth movement have produced so little on the subject.

One of the best examples of this strange oversight is in Terry Teykl's book **Pray and Grow**. Ezra Earl Jones, on behalf of the United Methodist Church of the United States, in his introduction to Teykl's book, lists that denomination's results of research into the 'top ten' factors for church growth. [24] Prayer does not even rate a mention!

The simplest answer to lack of growth in many churches may be that we have forgotten that the *'prayer of a righteous man is powerful and effective'* (James 5:16). Perhaps we do not have because we do not ask (James 4:2). Former chaplain of the United States Senate, Richard Halverson, advised that we really don't have any alternatives. He says, 'You can organise until you are exhausted; you can plan, programme and subsidise all your plans. But if you fail to pray, it is a waste of time. Prayer is not optional for us. It is mandatory. Not to pray is to disobey God.' [25]

In this book, a linkage between prayer and church growth will be explored, biblically, historically, and contemporaneously. It is hoped that this might be but one of many such investigations in the near future, which might contribute toward unravelling yet a little more of the 'mystery' of prayer and its relationship to growth of the church, which we need to see in greater measure than ever before.

Endnotes

1. James Marocco. 'Prayer Therapy,' *Church Growth*. June 1989, 16.
2. Paul E. Billheimer, *Destined for the Throne*. Fort Washington, Pennsylvania: Christian Literature Crusade, 1975, 43.
3. Dennis Lane, *When People Pray*. Singapore: Overseas Missionary Fellowship, 1987, 2.
4. Ian M. Hay, 'Uplifted Hands,' *SIM Now*. July/August 1990, 8.
5. Evan Davies, 'Where have All the Prayer Meetings Gone?' *New Life*, October 1989, 6.
6. George Peters, *Evangelical Missions Tomorrow*. Pasadena, California: William Carey Library Publications, 1977, 150.
7. Wesley L. Duewel, *Touch the World Through Prayer*. Grand Rapids, Michigan: Francis Ashbury Press, 1986, 13.
8. Bob J. Willhite, *Why Pray?* Altamonte Springs, Florida: Creation House, 1988, 15.
9. Dick Eastman, *The Hour That Changes the World*. Grand Rapids, Michigan: Baker, 1978, 5.
10. *Ibid.*, 171–74.
11. C. Peter Wagner, '1990: The Hinge Between Past and Future.' *Ministries Today*, May/June 1991, 32.
12. *Ibid.*
13. Peter Kuzmic, 'Pentecostal Fervour in Eastern Europe.' *World Missions Update*, October 1991, 3–4.
14. David Bryant, *Concerts of Prayer*. Ventura, California: Regal Books, 1984, 46.
15. *Ibid.*, 46–47.
16. *Australian Fellowship for Church Growth Bulletin* 4, April 1990: passim.
17. Harold Lindsell, 'Prayer and the Battle for the World.' In *Unleashing the Power of Prayer*, ed. Vonette Bright and Ben A. Jennings. Chicago: Moody Press, 1989, 294–96.
18. Billheimer, *Destined for the Throne*, 101
19. Ron Jensen and Jim Stevens, *Dynamics of Church Growth*. Grand Rapids, Michigan: Baker, 1981, 19.
20. Willhite, *Why Pray?* 111.

21. Elmer L. Towns, John N. Vaughan and David J. Serfert, *The Complete Book of Church Growth*. Wheaton, Illinois: Tyndale, 1981, 194.

22. Lee Lebsack, *10 at the Top: How 10 of America's Largest Assemblies of God Churches Grew*. Stowe, Ohio: New Hope Press, 1974, 94.

23. George Edgerly, *Survey of Pastors of 1974's Fastest Growing Schools*. Springfield, Missouri: Assemblies of God, n.d., 2.

24. Terry Teykl, *Pray and Grow*. Nashville, Tennessee: Discipleship Resources, 1988, v–vi.

25. Bryant, *Concerts of Prayer*, 39.

Chapter 1

Back to the Bible

A Strange Omission

After considerable exposure to church life in Great Britain and elsewhere, Dr Eddie Gibbs arrived at an important conclusion:

> 'As one studies case histories of growing churches there is one recurring factor – they are all praying churches. Around the British Isles ministers of growing churches in all denominations testify to the fact that it began as they met with those in their churches burdened by God to confess their spiritual apathy or impotence and to seek his power.' [1]

In the United States of America at Larry Lea's Church on the Rock in Rockwall, Texas, numerical growth was from thirteen people to eleven thousand in the period 1980–88. The story of how this happened is pieced together from his three books, [2] monthly columns in *Charisma* magazine and other outlets. His fundamental stance was 'I didn't start a church, I started a prayer meeting.' Among other things, he had a goal of enlisting 300,000 intercessors across America. Because of growth in his own church and his constant emphasis on prayer, he became known as 'God's chief apostle of prayer in America.'

At Second Baptist Church in Houston, Texas, Pastor Ed Young saw membership increase by two thousand in 1987. He claimed that nothing much was happening until their church became a 'house of prayer' in 1982. [3]

Dr Waymon Rogers of Evangel Christian Life Centre in Louisville, Kentucky, saw his membership decline from five hundred to two hundred people. Then God gave him a key to reverse the situation – prayer. He organised seven deacons to pray one hour per day and one hundred members formed a twenty-two hour per day prayer chain. The membership moved up to two thousand within two years. [4]

The fountainhead of this century's prayer movement, as it correlates to church growth, is Korea, where the Christian population has grown from 2 percent to 32 percent in the last three decades. In countless articles, and particularly in *Prayer: Key to Revival*, [5] Paul Yonggi Cho, senior minister of Yoido Full Gospel Church in Seoul, attributes that church's conversion rate of twelve thousand people per month and the whole continual revival situation primarily to ceaseless prayer.

Glen Sheppard, an outside observer, agrees. He says, 'The effectiveness of the Korean church is related to the intercessory prayer life of the people.' [6]

A preliminary survey of data and assessments would seem to indicate that particular prayer could be a powerful factor in church growth. Yet the intriguing thing is that in the vast majority of books on the subject of church growth, prayer is hardly considered. At best, it may rate a couple of pages in such works. Far more common is the fact that prayer may receive one or two references in the index, or no mention at all in many such volumes.

Peter Wagner sums up the scene well when he says, 'Prayer is a growth factor which has not been stressed nearly enough in church growth literature.' [7] Why is this so?

One can only guess. It may be because most of the literature on the subject has to date been generated by American researchers. Perhaps they selectively record and research only in areas in which they find personal interest. If so, it is understandable that prayer will not rate highly on the research-publication scale. Douglas and McNally found that American ministers spend only eight to nine minutes per day praying. [8]

Perhaps the scene was set by research inevitably following patterns established by the church growth movement's most influential founder, Donald McGavran. Tom Smail considers that

> 'one of the weaknesses of [McGavran's] work is that he tends to explain everything ... even to the point of suggesting that if we could know fully all the external circumstances at work in the situation, we could predict or engineer revival. In other words, he does not leave room for the properly spiritual factor.' [9]

Herbert Kane agrees. 'The proponents of church growth, with four exceptions, have emphasised the human factors and all but overlooked the divine factor,' [10] of which prayer would be a principal initiator.

In a field in which the superintendency of the Holy Spirit is presumably a dominant factor, [11] the lack of emphasis on and investigation of the role of prayer seems to be strange indeed.

In defence of those who work in the field, it needs to be said that church growth proponents try to uncover principles which facilitate or hinder growth. Even if such are discoverable, they can only explain and not cause growth or the lack of it. Whatever the cause of the apparent oversight in investigating prayer and its relationship to church growth, prayer itself remains an unquantifiable mystery which is essential if our knowledge of God is to remain based upon terms which are pleasing to him – that is, faith (Hebrews 11:6). [12]

To check further this seeming deficiency of research in the relationship of prayer and church growth, an interlibrary search of related titles was instituted by me in Melbourne, Australia in October 1988. Using the descriptors of 'Church

19

Growth', 'Prayer', 'Church', and 'Church Growth-Prayer', the following number of titles emerged:

Church Growth	534 titles
Prayer	1,672 titles
Church	60,341 titles
Church Growth-Prayer	1 title
	(by Dudley and Cummings)[13]

Whatever the explanation for the comparative lack of major research and reporting done in this area, the situation needs to be redressed. Also, we need to move behind the rhetoric of believing in prayer to actually doing the work of prayer.

In both regards the tide may be turning. Dr Duncan McIntosh, director for Church Growth and Evangelism programmes for the Home Mission Board of American Baptist Churches, said that their church growth programme began with prayer.

'For us the key for all growth lies in the prayer life ... If you don't have a prayer emphasis for the church the planning will be just organisational and routine. If we are going to understand what the church is to be and to be driven by the urgency needed, we must be in conversation with the head of the church.'[14]

Some Definitions

Prayer

Hallesby defines prayer as 'an attitude of our hearts, an attitude of our minds ... toward God.'[15] It arises out of our helplessness which causes us to put our faith in God.[16] The problem with this definition is its anthropocentricity. Hallesby is not alone in this trend. Dick Eastman offers fifteen definitions of prayer, fourteen of which are similarly anthropocentric.[17] Elsewhere, the Almighty seems to have acknowledged active access to the process, in that the person who prays is encouraged at least to listen. [18]

To define prayer more adequately, we ought to move beyond those definitions which place ourselves at the centre of our own constructed universe, and acknowledge that it is an activity which mentally, emotionally, and spiritually engages at least two living beings, otherwise it is only soliloquous self-talk.

Again, the activist, materialist West which insists on endless talk and the aggressive postulation of our (superior?) opinions and positions, has much to learn from the more meditative, reflective East in understanding and practising prayer. Could it be that the deficiencies of our cultural drive reflect in the fact that American pastors pray only twenty-two minutes per day, while those in Japan, Korea, and China pray 44, 90, and 120 minutes per day respectively (which correlates with respective national church growth patterns in these countries)? [19]

Prayer at least needs to incorporate the interdependent polarities of speaking and listening (John 5:19, 30; 14:26; 16:24). If nothing is ever heard or received then what is the point of it all? Our spirituality may be little more than a reflection of cultural factors which are the summation of millions of dominant personalities, one of the characteristics of which is a diminished willingness to listen. In that Rosalind Rinker's book made just this point, and was reprinted 18 times in its first eight years, this would seem to be a welcome revelation to many. She sees prayer as dialogue between two persons who love each other. [20]

We would do well to heed the ancient admonition of Ecclesiastes 5:2:

> *'Do not be quick with your mouth,*
> *do not be hasty in your heart*
> *to utter anything before God.*
> *God is in heaven*
> *and you are on earth*
> *so let your words be few.'*

Unless such advice is heeded, we will experience the truth of an ancient American Indian proverb, 'Listen, or your tongue will keep you deaf.'

It may well be the personal inadequacies of purchasing power or the stocking policies of local Christian book-stores, but of the more than forty books on prayer owned by me, only two address the listening aspect of prayer in any major way.[21] The same Christian book-stores also report that books on prayer are the slowest selling line.

The simplest definition may be that prayer is effective communication between God and man.[22]

Church Growth

The 'science' of church growth is still too new for normative definitions to have been developed. The discovery of all the factors involved and our ability to measure, relate and inter-pret them consistently is still some time away. However, any working definition will have to take into account indices of quantity (Matthew 28:18–20), quality (Acts 2:42–43), and organisational complexity (e.g., Acts 6:1–7; 13:1–3).

Cheney and Lewis have a reasonably inclusive grasp of the current state of progress when they classify church growth into four categories.[23]

1. Quality or internal growth

This takes place when a church is edified and growing in grace toward Christian maturity. It may be termed teleologi-cal growth. It often results in and from evangelism among the children of church members. Apart from this, at this stage, this type of growth remains largely unmeasurable. One of the primary causes for the writing of the epistles was to produce this type of growth (1 Corinthians 2:6; 3:1; 13:11; Ephesians 4:14; Philippians 3:15; Hebrews 5:14; 6:1).

2. Expansion growth

This is within a community and occurs mostly from evangel-ism when converts are won from the same cultural or social group as the evangelising church.

3. Extension growth

This describes church planting, that is, when a mother church establishes a branch or daughter church in another community. Again, it is mostly the product of evangelism within the same cultural or social group.

4. Bridging (or commissioning) growth

This occurs when churches are planted within communities which, compared with the originating church or community, are significantly different in terms of culture, race, language and/or socioeconomic status. It may result from evangelism in which the target people are significantly but not totally different from the sending church, or from evangelism in which the target community is totally different from the witnessing community.

Expansion, extension, and bridging growth will also necessitate growth in organisational complexity.

Growth – A Supernatural Process

In that the church, a living organism, is God's creation with Jesus Christ as its head (Colossians 1:18) from whom life flows (John 14:6), then any sort of true and lasting growth is going to be a supernatural process. Man has a part to play in planting the seed of the gospel and watering it, but Paul well understood that the process was supernatural when he placed the emphasis and responsibility for growth where it can only be – with God (1 Corinthians 3:6). In this he was doing no more than reiterating the sentiments of the Psalmist several centuries earlier, who also acknowledged that

> *'unless the Lord builds the house, its builders labour in vain.'* (Psalm 127:1) [24]

We might have excellent leadership, organisational structures, preaching and teaching programmes, or suchlike, but these of themselves do not produce growth. In fact the very devices we use for measuring health and growth in a church, for example, offerings, attendances or physical plant, may mislead us into thinking we are seeing growth when we are not. God's measurements for such are often different from ours, as is clearly shown in the comparative perceptions of growth for the churches at Ephesus (Revelation 2:1–4) and Sardis (Revelation 3:1–3).

The transfer of a soul from the kingdom of darkness to that of light (Colossians 1:13) is a spiritual, supernatural process. It is the Father who draws (John 6:44). It is the Holy Spirit who convicts (John 16:8–11), causes confession to be made (1 Corinthians 12:3), and completes conversion (Titus 3:5).

It is the Holy Spirit who also strengthens and empowers (Ephesians 3:16), guides into Truth (John 16:16), and gives spiritual gifts which promote unity (1 Corinthians 12:25) and build up the church (1 Corinthians 14:12), thus avoiding disunity and strife which stunt growth.

It is he who does these things as signs for unbelievers (1 Corinthians 14:22) which cause repentance in them (1 Corinthians 14:24), thus accelerating cycles of growth. Similarly, he is the cause of spiritual fruit (Galatians 5:22), especially that of love (1 Corinthians 13), which is the very essence of God (1 John 4:8), which again attracts the unbeliever (John 13:34–35) from death to life (John 5:24). It is the Lord of the church who aims for maturity and growth (Philippians 1:6), who through the Spirit appoints officers (Ephesians 4:11),

'... so that the body of Christ may be built up, until we all reach unity in the faith and in the knowledge of the Son of God and become mature, attaining to the whole measure of the fullness of Christ.'   (Ephesians 4:12–13)

This is indisputable, fundamental, spiritual truth which is accepted and believed by all Christians. However, the degree to which we are convinced that all real growth is ultimately a supernatural process and are prepared to act upon that belief, will be directly reflected in the priority that we give to corporate and personal prayer in the life of the church.

It is only 'when we begin to see that nothing that matters will occur except in answer to prayer, that prayer will become more than an optional programme for the faithful few, and instead will become [the] driving force of our churches.'[25]

'God wants our churches, our pastors and our leaders to recognise that only he can do extraordinary things. When we accept that simple premise, we will begin to pray,'[26] and that will change us and our churches as prayer takes its rightful place as the foundation for church growth.

Dependent on Prayer

The priority of prayer as a pattern for power was established early in the history of Israel. For example, in Israel's battle with the Amalekites, it was Joshua who was on the plain leading the Israelite army forward. But the lesson drawn from this event is quite simple and clear: Joshua's prevailing on his battlefield below was directly dependent upon Moses' prayerful intercession from on top of his nearby hill with the support of Aaron and Hur (Exodus 17:8–13).

No matter how propitious the factors of the physical environment appeared to be, to act without explicit instructions so to do from the Lord himself could lead to disaster (Deuteronomy 1:44–45). To do the otherwise impossible and possess the land against all odds, a right relationship with God was required. If this was not maintained, then the advance would be stalled with consequent suffering and tragedy befalling God's people (Joshua 7).

When the relationship was restored and his voice was clearly heard and obeyed, the same situation was reversed with attendant blessing and rapid success (Joshua 8:1–28). Only as the people recovenanted to return to humble themselves and to pray and seek God, could personal, national and international adversity be overcome (2 Chronicles 7:14).

The priority on prayer is stressed even further in the New

Testament, which is not surprising, with Jesus' emphasis on the preeminence of One who was henceforth to be known as Father – especially in prayer (Matthew 6:9; Luke 11:2). Such is expressive of a relationship which progresses towards and deepens in intimacy, the more time is given to it. Bingham Hunter identifies no fewer than 290 references to prayer in the New Testament, whereas in the Old Testament, excluding the special nature of the Psalms, he identifies only 77 explicit references to prayer. [27] As would be expected, the watershed of emphasis occurred with the person and ministry of Jesus. Of the 102 identifiable references to prayer in the Gospels alone, 94 relate directly to Jesus. [28] These may be categorised as follows:

12 prayers of Jesus
25 references to prayer in Jesus' life
27 references to petition/prayers addressed to Jesus
30 references to Jesus teaching about prayer
 8 other references to prayer.

Clearly prayer is meant to assume a position of personal and corporate prominence and importance, hitherto unrecorded in God's dealing with and expectations of his people.

Paul frequently re-emphasises the priority:

'I want men everywhere to lift up holy hands in prayer.'
(1 Timothy 2:8)

'I urge then, first of all, that . . . , prayers . . . be made for everyone.' (1 Timothy 2:1)

'. . . in everything, by prayer . . . , present your requests to God.' (Philippians 4:6)

'Pray continually; . . . for this is God's will for you.'
(1 Thessalonians 5:17–18)

Obviously for Paul, as with Jesus, 'Prayer was the highest exercise in his personal life [and] assumed the same high place in his teaching ... [and] practice.' [29] He also applied the same primary, exacting imperative to individuals and the church through his repeated admonitions. According to his understanding, this is explicitly God's will for his church.

Other New Testament writers agree. Peter urges believers to be clear minded and self controlled – so that they can pray (1 Peter 4:7). James declares that prayer is powerful and effective (James 5:16). John assures us that God hears (and answers) (1 John 5:15).

Prayer and Church Growth in Acts

The book of Acts deserves special attention because although it reads primarily as a documentation of the church's foundation and development, it is not just secular history as we understand such in the West today. It is sacred history repeatedly drawing attention to, and inviting interpretation of, God's intervention in the affairs of man. As such, therefore, the events take on theological significance.

It is also not surprising then that the medium facilitating divine-human interaction was that of prayer.

'[The book of Acts] in its deepest sense is the record of the acts of the risen Christ performed by the apostles, in the power of the Holy Spirit ... Followers of Christ looked upon themselves as the agents of a higher Power ... With that higher Power they kept in unbroken connection through prayer.

The early church was a praying church as well as a working church; and it was a working church because it was a praying church. As soon as it was born it began to pray; and it grew in strength and efficiency as its prayer life developed.' [30]

'None can deny the prayer factor in the early church.' [31]

There was prayer:

1. Preceding the outpouring of the Holy Spirit (Acts 1:14)
2. At the first miracle of Peter and John (Acts 3:1–10)
3. At the first incident of persecution (Acts 4:23–31)
4. When Peter's life was under threat (Acts 12:5) and
5. At the establishment of each new church (Acts 14:23).

According to my analysis, [32] there are thirty-seven references to or instances of prayer, as previously defined, within the twenty-eight chapters of Acts. Bingham Hunter claims forty references. [33]

There are also, according to my analysis, thirty-six references to church growth, as previously defined, in the same book. However, not all instances of church growth are related to references to prayer, or vice versa. Of the 36 references to church growth, 58 percent (i.e., twenty-one instances) are within the context of prayer. Of the 21 references linking prayer and church growth, 8 refer to quantitative growth, while 13 relate to other sorts of growth.

Although there are 15 instances of growth without reference to prayer, a case may be established that while one may pray and not necessarily see church growth, it is highly improbable that any significant growth of any description will or can occur without recourse to prayer. This is to be expected when it is remembered that in the enterprise of church growth, as in other church activities, our relationship to God is well described not as sole owners but as co-workers (1 Corinthians 3:9; 2 Corinthians 6:1). 'God has chosen to accomplish many of His sovereign purposes with our help ... [He] has appointed us to a sacred partnership for the purpose of gospel advance.' [34] We could not have even begun to attain and maintain that status were it not for prayer, perhaps by others (Matthew 9:38; Luke 10:2).

Melvin Hodges says, 'The importance of prayer in establishing a church and maintaining its life can scarcely be over-estimated. Prayer links pastor and people with the living head of the church ... Prayer makes this partnership a reality.' [35]

Of particular interest is the pattern, quality, and precedents of prayer established by the foundation of the church. Acts 1:14 says,

'They were all joined together constantly in prayer . . . '

'All joined together' (*omothumadon*) means with one mind or purpose, with one accord. That is the 'prerequisite [for] effectiveness.' [36]

To fulfil a prerequisite is one thing. To carry it through to effectiveness is another. But that is precisely what the earliest church excelled at. *'They were all joined together constantly in prayer.'* The word which the NIV translates 'constantly' is *proskarterountes*, which means 'to be busily engaged in, to be devoted to.' [37] It also similarly means 'to persist in adhering to a thing, to be intently engaged in, to attend to constantly.' [38] Here the word is in the form of a present participle, which implies 'repetition, incompleteness [and] continuance.' [39]

The writer of Acts used exactly the same word and part of speech in Acts 2:42, again in relation to the church, prayer and growth. Here is a linkage established from the beginning which was meant to be continuously pursued because neither the need for prayer, nor the growth of the church can ever be completed until our Lord returns.

It is hardly any surprise, therefore, that Paul used exactly the same word in relation to prayer in Colossians 4:2, except that he used it in the present imperative form (*proskartereite*). The practice of the early church of devoting themselves to prayer continually became not just a matter to be considered, but a command to be obeyed!

Bridging (or commissioning) growth within the environment of prayer is especially evidenced in Acts as follows:

Acts 9:10–16	Ananias to Saul
Acts 9:20	Saul
Acts 13:2–3	Saul and Barnabas
Acts 16:6–10	Paul and party to Macedonia
Acts 22:6–21	Paul recounts his own commissioning
Acts 23:11	Paul to Rome

Bridging growth is necessary to complete the task of world evangelisation. Bryant advances five aspects, the process of which also demonstrates the interwovenness of prayer with this category of church growth: [40]

1. World Evangelisation is from beginning to end the work of God (Colossians 1:17–23).

2. Therefore only he can awaken the church to renewed zeal for Christ (Ephesians 1:16–23).

3. The church pursues God's work of awakening and world evangelisation through united, concerted, sustained prayer (Ephesians 6:16–20)

4. ... to the fulfilment of his global cause of evangelisation (Matthew 6:9–13).

5. Such a movement of united prayer is normally initiated by pioneers of faith who embrace God's redemptive purpose and set the pace (Acts 4:23–31).

As would be expected, the principle and practice, deliberately or intuitively, was taken from Acts into later generations of church experience so that no matter which of the biographies of the pioneers or founders of even modern mission movements one consults – William Carey, Adoniram Judson, David Livingston, Hudson Taylor, or whomever – the initiating thrust of the work of their lives began in prayer encounters.

The principle is evidenced not only in the practice of outstanding founding pioneers, but in whole movements which grew up behind them. For example, one of the major expansions in the cross-cultural workforce which occurred in the nineteenth century became known as the Student Christian Federation. Its base was among college and university students. It supplied twenty thousand career missionaries in the space of thirty years. Its leader, John R. Mott 'found that the source of this awakening lay in united intercessory prayer.' [41]

Just as prayer was vital for the selection and commissioning of such workers (Matthew 9:38; Luke 10:2; Acts 13:2), it was seen to be of equal importance in sustaining the worker and in maintaining and expanding the work. Thus Paul asked for prayer for:

1. His protection and for acceptance of his ministry (Romans 15:31)
2. Boldness in proclamation (Ephesians 6:19)
3. Open doors so he could present the gospel (Colossians 4:2–3)
4. The rapid spread of the gospel (2 Thessalonians 3:1–2).

'It is obvious that the entire church-planting operation is to be continually bathed in believing prayer.'[42]

Hudson Taylor once told of a missionary couple in charge of ten stations who felt it necessary to write to their Home Secretary confessing their lack of progress. The suggestion was made that the Secretary try to find ten persons, each of whom would take one station as a special object of unceasing prayer.

As time passed, in seven of the ten mission stations much of the opposition began to melt away. It was replaced by spiritual revival and significant numbers came to Christ. However, in the other three areas, there was no change. Again the missionary wrote to the Secretary expressing bewilderment over the lack of growth of the three. It did not take the Secretary long to clear up the mystery. He had succeeded in getting special intercessors for seven of the ten stations, but not for the other three.[43]

That is why S.D. Gordon said, 'The greatest thing anyone can do for God and man is to pray.'[44]

From the times of the Acts of the Apostles through almost two millennia of the Christian era, the principle of prayer married to the practice of outreach has produced similar results – qualitative, quantifiable, observable, church growth.

Endnotes

1. Eddie Gibbs, *I Believe in Church Growth*. London: Hodder and Stoughton, 1981, 135–36.
2. Larry Lea, *Could You Not Tarry One Hour?* Altamonte Springs, Florida: Creation House, 1987; *Praying with Jesus*. Altamonte

Springs, Florida: Creation House, 1987; *The Hearing Ear*. Altamonte Springs, Florida: Creation House, 1988.

3. C. Peter Wagner, *Intercession for Christian Leaders*. Church Growth II lecture, Pasadena: August, 1988.

4. Lee Lebsack, *10 at the Top. How 10 of America's Largest Assemblies of God Churches Grew*. Stowe, Ohio: New Hope Press, 1974, 30–35.

5. Paul Y. Cho, *Prayer: Key to Revival*. Waco, Texas: Word, 1984.

6. Glen Sheppard, 'Prayer for Spiritual Awakening,' *Decision*, March 1988, 12.

7. C. Peter Wagner, *Leading Your Church to Growth*. Ventura, California: Regal, 1984, 198.

8. Merril E. Douglas and Joyce McNally, 'How Ministers Use Their Time,' *The Christian Ministry*, January 1980, 23.

9. Tom Smail, *The Forgotten Father*. London: Hodder and Stoughton, 1980, 78–79.

10. J. Herbert Kane, *The Christian Mission Today and Tomorrow*. Grand Rapids: Baker, 1981, 212.

11. See George W. Peters, *A Theology of Church Growth*. Grand Rapids: Zondervan, 1981, 140.

12. See Terry Muck, *Liberating the Leader's Prayer Life*. Waco, Texas: Word, 1985, 56.

13. Roger L. Dudley and Des Cummings, 'A Study of Factors Relating to Church Growth in the North American Division of Seventh Day Adventists,' *Review of Religious Research*, 24, June 1983, 322–33.

14. Duncan McIntosh, 'Prayer is the Key to Church Growth,' *The Victorian Baptist Witness*, August 1990, 4.

15. O. Hallesby, *Prayer*. London: Inter-Varsity Press, 1965, 13.

16. *Ibid.*, 13–28.

17. Dick Eastman, *Change the World School of Prayer*. Penshurst, Australia: World Literature Crusade, 1983, 12–16.

18. Dick Eastman, *The Hour that Changes the World*. Grand Rapids, Michigan: Baker, 1978, 127–34.

19. C. Peter Wagner, Preliminary research undertaken and discussed in *Church Growth II*, Pasadena, 1988; cf. Douglas and McNally, n. 8 above.

20. Rosalind Rinker, *Prayer. Conversing with God*. Grand Rapids, Michigan: Zondervan, 1959, 23.

21. Lea, *The Hearing Ear*; Mark Virkler, *Dialogue with God*. Woy Woy, NSW: Peacemakers, 1987.

22. See Sheppard, 'Prayer for Spiritual Awakening,' 12.

23. Charles L. Chaney and Ron S. Lewis, *Design for Church Growth*. Nashville, Tennessee: Broadman, 1977, 19–22.

24. See Ron Jenson and Jim Stevens, *Dynamics of Church Growth*. Grand Rapids, Michigan: Baker 1981, 19.

25. *Ibid.*, 27.

26. *Ibid.*, 30.

27. W. Bingham Hunter, *The God Who Hears*. Downers Grove, Illinois: Inter-Varsity Press, 1986, 204–7.

28. *Ibid.*, 202–4.

29. E.M. Bounds, *Prayer and Praying Men*. Grand Rapids, Michigan: Baker, 1977, 109.

30. James M. Campbell, *The Place of Prayer in the Christian Religion*. New York: The Methodist Book Concern, 1915, 137.

31. Reginald Klimionok, *Levels of Church Growth*. Slacks Creek, Queensland: Assembly Press, 1984, 179.

32. See Appendix 1.

33. Hunter, *The God Who Hears*, 206.

34. Wesley L. Duewel, *Touch the World Through Prayer*. Grand Rapids, Michigan: Francis Ashbury Press, 1986, 22.

35. Melvin L. Hodges, *A Guide to Church Planting*. Chicago: Moody Press, 1973, 65.

36. E.M. Blaiklock, *Acts*. London: Tyndale, 1959, 52.

37. W.F. Arndt and F.W. Gingrich, *A Greek English Lexicon*. Chicago: University of Chicago Press, 1957, 722.

38. Samuel Bagster, *The Analytical Greek Lexicon*. London: Samuel Bagster and Sons, 1967, 350.

39. Eric G. Jay, *New Testament Greek*. London: SPCK, 1961, 166.

40. David Bryant, *Concerts of Prayer*. Ventura, California: Regal Books, 1985, 41.

41. *Ibid.*, 40.

42. J. Hesselgrave, *Planting Churches Cross-Culturally*. Grand Rapids, Michigan: Baker, 1978, 144.

43. 'Prayer the Greatest Thing,' *Australia's New Day*, April 1983, 40.

44. *Ibid.*

Chapter 2

The Tough Stuff

Fasting

Locust plagues were well known to Minnesota farmers. Their crops had been destroyed by the voraciously hungry insects in the summer of 1876. Now in the spring of 1877 they waited and watched to see whether such pestilence would strike yet again. If it did the farming future of thousands of families would be wiped out – permanently.

Acutely aware of the impending disaster Governor J.S. Pillsbury proclaimed that April 26 would be a day of prayer and fasting to plead with God to save them from calamity. The Governor urged that every single person should unite and participate toward this end.

Across the state people responded to their Governor's call. In gatherings large and small Minnesotans assembled to fast and pray.

The very next day as the sun soared in a cloudless sky, with temperatures also rising, the people noticed to their dismay that the dreaded insects started to stir in the warmed soil.

For three more days the uninterrupted unseasonal heat caused a vast army of locusts to hatch. It was of such plague proportions as to threaten the entire North-West farm sector. Then as the sun departed at the end of that fourth day, with the locusts all hatched and ready to move, a sudden climatic

35

change flicked a blanket of frost across the entire area where the locusts waited for dawn and take-off. Most were killed right where they crouched. Come summer, instead of scorched stubbled dirt, as far as the eye could see, the wheat crop waved in golden glory. In the history of Minnesota, April 26, 1877 is recorded as the day when God wonderfully responded to the prayers and fasting of his people.

Almost a century later, at least one Minnesotan remembered the powerful combination of persistent prayer within the context of fasting. In a south Asian city when he saw a cow about to be slaughtered in front of a mosque, during the Muslim festival of Eid ul Adha, he stopped his car, took a few pictures, then drove on home. But that night the Holy Spirit began to challenge him to be less a tourist and more a missionary. He was directed to commence praying and fasting, to return to the scene of the sacrifice and to be a witness to the greater sacrifice of Jesus.

In the steaming pre-monsoon heat of the next day, he set off with his shoulder bag full of tracts and gospels to the same place in the bazaar, where he had taken the pictures the preceding day near the mosque. Having sold and distributed much, as he returned home he felt well satisfied that he had done his 'duty'. But the Holy Spirit impressed upon him that night that he was to continue his praying and fasting and to return to repeat the process in the same place the next day. Night after night as the missionary prayed the Holy Spirit repeated his instruction to his obedient servant.

It didn't take long for local opposition to form and even threaten his life. He was dragged through the market place, doused in dye, kicked and pushed into a dirty ditch and stoned. Twice a fanatic tried to kill him with a dagger but was restrained by his own people.

Finally, two well trained rabble rousers were appointed to stop his witnessing. They approached him directly, warning him that should he return again he wouldn't leave the bazaar alive.

On the fortieth day of this supernaturally sustained period of prayer and fasting, directed by what the Spirit was saying, he bade what he thought could be his final farewell to his wife and set out once more with his literature to sell and distribute in the bazaar. No sooner had he arrived than the appointed crowd conductors also showed up. They tore up his gospels and his tracts and began to incite the growing crowd which quickly gathered to watch the spectacle. Soon there were calls to kill him.

Then, just as men moved in to grab him, two unusually tall strangers appeared. Spearing a path through the crowd which was now calling for the missionary's blood, in one swift move, they grabbed the missionary, removed him from the crush of people and took him down a laneway at the end of which was a waiting bicycle rickshaw.

Amazingly, no one had followed them.

Placing the missionary in the rickshaw, the strangers said to him, 'It is enough for now. Don't come back.' God's messengers had saved his servant. That night the Lord spoke once more saying. 'Now you know how much I love and care for Muslims. It is not my will that any of them should perish without hearing the message of salvation.'

With no other tangible resources, other than the practice of sustained prayer and fasting, that missionary went on to be used of God literally to build what became one of the largest churches in that somewhat hostile environment.

When Christians combine prayer with fasting, powerful spiritual forces seem to be harnessed and released. Hence 'no study of prayer (and its relationship to church growth) could ever be complete without a careful look at the importance of fasting...' [1]

Today in the western church, fasting is hardly a widespread or fashionable spiritual discipline. In fact, there is ample evidence to suggest that the practice of the opposite, overeating, may be more widespread. Physical overweight is common even among church leaders.

While fasting has become a political mechanism in many countries, or even a means of fundraising through sponsorships of some well known charities, it is either ignored or mentioned only jokingly in large sections of the church. In others it receives institutionalised, seasonal, partial attention in perhaps periods prior to Easter. Even though it is also acceptable for practitioners of that other great 'religion' of our times, professional sport, for boxers, jockeys and others to be expected to fast to reduce body weight to reach required limits before their respective events, mostly, at least in well fed western societies, fasting is often regarded as something of a far removed medieval monastic religious discipline or that which may be practised in other contemporary non-Christian religions.

For many Christians, Ephesians 5:29 is literally true:

> *'No one ever hated his own body, but he feeds and cares for it . . . '*

Be that as it may, we would be unwise to dismiss it simply because it was currently unpopular or relatively neglected.

What is fasting? For our purposes it may be defined as 'the voluntary deliberate abstinence from food for the purpose of concentrated prayer.' [2]

It was a spiritual exercise known and practised from Israel's earliest times. For example:

Moses fasted for forty days, twice (Deuteronomy 9:9, 18).

Joshua fasted after defeat at Ai (Joshua 7:6).

From time to time all Israel was called to fast (Judges 20:26; 1 Samuel 7:6).

From its historical experience, Israel knew that prayer within the context of fasting wrought particularly potent spiritual victories which impacted upon the realm of the physical. For example:

King Jehosaphat won a large battle without engaging in physical combat (2 Chronicles 20:1–30).

Ezra obtained safe passage (Ezra 8:21–23).

Esther was used to transform potential genocide into national salvation (Esther 4:16).

Pagan Nineveh was spared while Samaria was destroyed (Jonah 3:5–9).

In the New Testament era, although we are not under the law of the Old Testament but in the age of grace, nevertheless Jesus teaches about fasting for those who would become his followers. In the famous Sermon on the Mount (Matthew 6:1–18) Jesus refers to three related responsibilities:

giving,

praying and

fasting.

On these religious responsibilities Jesus presents them more as an assumed obligation rather than an option. He did not say 'If you give ... pray ... or fast' but rather

'when you give ... when you pray ... when you fast.'

In Matthew 6:16 he spoke in the plural collective sense, while in the two verses immediately following (vs. 17–18) he addressed the singular or individual practice. Thus in the church which was yet to be, it would have both corporate and private significance.

Jesus not only taught about fasting, he also practised it. Luke says that when Jesus was already *'full of the Holy Spirit'* (Luke 4:1) he was then led out into the desert where he prayed and fasted through an encounter with Satan. Then *'he returned in the power of the Spirit'* (Luke 4:14). He started out 'full' of the Spirit and in part as a result of his prayer and fasting, he became 'empowered' by the Spirit.

Having exemplified it in his own ministry, Jesus went on to stress its necessity to achieve spiritual breakthroughs when prayer by itself proved inadequate (Mark 9:29).

The Pharisees of the day fasted, as did the disciples of John the Baptist. So widespread did the practice seem, that onlookers were surprised when they noticed Jesus' disciples weren't fasting. He defended them by equating his presence with that of a bridal celebration, but clearly inferred that following his departure, his disciples certainly would fast (Mark 2:18–20).

In the early church, prayer and fasting were the means by which the first missionary personnel were identified and commissioned (Acts 13:1–3). Additionally these combined practices played a significant role in the establishment of churches and the appointment of their respective leadership teams, thereby securing better their future further growth (Acts 14:21–23).

The Apostle Paul also resorted to these twin spiritual resources immediately upon his conversion and prior to his commissioning and commencement of his own ministry (Acts 9:9). Later he referred to fasting as a sign of the legitimacy of his missionary ministry (2 Corinthians 6:3–10; 11:23–27).

Throughout the Old Testament era and in the New in the ministries of Jesus, the Apostle Paul and the early Church, fasting was a normative practice. Furthermore, it did not cease with the death of the Church Fathers. According to Epiphanius, Bishop of Salamis, in the fourth century, fasting was still the universal, habitual practice of all Christians on Wednesdays and Fridays of each week.

Reformers Luther, Calvin, Knox and Latimer all practised prayer with fasting and claimed an increased resultant effectiveness in their respective ministries. Wesley was so impressed by such precedents that he would not even ordain a person to ministry unless that person agreed to fast at least until 4.00 p.m. each Wednesday and Friday. [3]

In America when well known evangelist, Jonathan Edwards, sensed he was not seeing the spiritual breakthroughs he thought were appropriate, he fasted and prayed continuously for three days and nights. Over and over again he was heard praying, 'Give me New England. Give me New England.' When he finally arose from his knees and made his way into the pulpit, the people gazed at him as if they could almost see the face of God. When he began to speak, immediately conviction fell upon his audience. Like Jesus, prior to prayer and fasting, Edwards was full of the Spirit. Now he was extraordinarily empowered by the Spirit and it showed in the visible results of his evangelistic ministry.

The church which has seen the greatest and most sustained growth this century would probably be that of Korea. As

will be seen later, extraordinary prayer is one of the funda-
mentals of faith and practice throughout the Korean church.
But far more frequently than in the Western church, in
Korea, prayer is also linked to fasting. That nation's well
known pastor, Paul Y. Cho says:

> 'Normally I teach my people to begin to fast for three
> days. Once they have become accustomed to three day
> fasts they will be able to fast for a period of seven days;
> then, they will move to ten day fasts. Some have even
> gone for forty days but this is usually not encouraged.'[4]

So what happens when believers fast?

Firstly, some suggest that firstly true fasting, emotionally
and spiritually, is a form of mourning.

However, this ought not to be confused with mourning in
the more common human sense which is often within the
context of blackness and despair. Godly fasting is something
different.

Jesus said that after his departure his people would fast
because as it is with a bridegroom leaving, there would be
sadness (Matthew 9:15). But that fasting would eventually
be replaced by feasting (Revelation 22:17, 20). Fasting
which is prompted by the Holy Spirit helps us to identify
with God's grief over the sin and folly of humanity. We are
sharing God's feelings.

Jesus said,

> *'Blessed are they that mourn.'*   (Matthew 5:4)

Elsewhere we are promised that there will be

> '...*beauty for ashes, the oil of joy for mourning, the
> garment of praise for the spirit of heaviness.'*
> (Isaiah 61:3)

Recently, as I was praying alone early one morning, I was
suddenly made to realise to what degree my church had been

subjected to gossip, ridicule and laughter because we dared to believe that at such a time of national economic depression God wanted us to do something extraordinary. In the midst of such gloom he was wanting us to plan and prepare for victory and expansion.

As I became aware of these things, it seemed to me that I personally had become the recipient of the scorn, scoffing, derision and slander. I started to weep, not so much feeling sorry for myself, but feeling how God feels when any part of His body is so regarded. I sensed I was moving into a different realm of the Spirit, touching the father heart of God as we communed for the next hour or so.

Secondly, when we fast we are bringing our physical bodies into submission.

In 1 Corinthians 9:27 Paul said:

> *'I beat my body and make it my slave so that after I have preached to others, I myself will not be disqualified for the prize.'*

Paul kept his body under subjection. It is said of fire that it is a wonderful servant but a terrible master. The same could be said of bodies. So each time we fast we are showing our bodies who is in charge. In effect we are saying, 'Body, stomach, fleshly appetites, you will serve me. I will not be dominated by you.' In Galatians 5:7 Paul writes:

> *'The sinful nature desires what is contrary to the Spirit, and the Spirit what is contrary to sinful nature. They are in conflict with each other.'*

Intimately connected to our sinful nature is our 'flesh'. It is through our flesh that sin comes enticing us. Fasting deals with the two great barriers which are erected by our own carnal natures. These are the self-will of the soul and the insistent self-gratifying appetites of our bodies.

Rightly practised, fasting brings both soul and body into submission to the Holy Spirit. Barriers are broken down, communion is opened up. Fasting does not change God, his purposes, plans or standards. But it does change us.

In 2 Samuel 12 is recorded the story of King David's adultery with Bathsheba. As a result of that act a child was conceived and born. But God decreed that the child would die. The child did die. God did not change but David certainly did. He came to an attitude of repentance and then God was able to forgive him.

Thirdly, when we fast we ought to expect to be victorious overcomers in the matter upon which our accompanying prayer is focused.

2 Chronicles 20: 1–30 is the story of what happened when King Jehoshaphat was faced with a hostile army invading his territory from the east. He lacked resources adequate to meet the threat. Therefore

> *'he proclaimed a fast throughout Judah. He gathered together all the people so that they might ask God's help.'*   (2 Chronicles 20:3–4)

Jehaziel led the people in singing and praising God. Israel did not have to engage the enemy in hand to hand contact. The invaders self-destructed. So sweeping and startling was Israel's victory that no other nation dared to attack them for years to come. Collective fasting was a high priority element employed in the spiritual area to gain supremacy in the realm of the physical.

Paul highlights this principle when he says,

> *'The weapons we fight with are not the weapons of the world. On the contrary, they have divine power to demolish strongholds.'*   (2 Corinthians 10:4)

His spiritual weapons include united prayer combined with fasting.

When Jesus' disciples asked him why they couldn't be as effective as him in ministry, he replied that some things are achieved *'only by prayer and fasting'* (Mark 9:29). Victory is achieved firstly in the realm of the spiritual and then follows that in the physical.

Fourthly, we fast so that we may be heard in heaven.

When Ezra faced the difficult assignment of leading his people through dangerous territory from their place of exile back to their own land, so that they might know how to proceed and receive God's favour and protection, he proclaimed a fast (Ezra 8:21–23). The result was that throughout their long trek through hostile areas they were neither molested by bandits nor attacked by savage tribes. They suffered no loss of property or persons because they had been heard and were protected from on high.

Similarly, when the Jewish nation faced its greatest crisis through a decreed threat of annihilation in the days of King Xerxes, Esther requested Mordecai to *'gather together all the Jews who are in Susa, and fast . . . '* (Esther 4:16). The outcome was that in spite of the overwhelming odds against them, the Jewish people were all spared and their enemy was destroyed in a sudden remarkable reversal of royal edicts.

If the principles and the outcomes are timeless, then as we might expect, they will not be confined only to Bible times.

In 1991 Peru's much feared Shining Path guerilla terrorist group issued a death threat against that nation's national director of Every Home Contact, Filipe Ortiz. 'Stop the work or pay the price with your life,' they said. Through a method of tract distribution, Christian workers had been winning the battle for the hearts and minds of people, especially in Ayacucho province which was a Shining Path stronghold. Ortiz called for protective prayer cover (and fasting) for himself and his teams. In the next two years even though they travelled to the remotest villages on foot and known guerillas and drug traffickers were in their audiences as they continued to preach and distribute their literature, no harm came to them from any source, including Peru's most feared Shining Path group. [5]

Fifthly, we fast to seek revelation regarding the will of God.

Being heard in heaven is only half of the process for those

of us who minister on earth. Obviously if the kingdom of God and the will of God is to be *'done on earth as it is in heaven'* (Matthew 6:10), those of us who are instruments of its coming need to know the will of the Father and be willing to act accordingly.

In Acts 13:2–3 there is the account of believers in Antioch praying, fasting and worshipping the Lord. It was in that context that the Holy Spirit chose to make known his will regarding missionary outreach and who was to lead it, Barnabas and Saul.

In Daniel 9 there is the well known story of Daniel waiting before God for revelation. He

> *'turned to the Lord God and pleaded with him in prayer and petition, in fasting . . . '* (Daniel 9:3)

Eventually Gabriel was able to reach him and advise,

> *'Daniel, I have now come to give you insight and understanding.'* (Daniel 9:22)

These biblical stories do not provide guarantees that fasting must always result in such clear spiritual guidance. But it would seem that by fasting at least 'we place ourselves in a situation that allows the Holy Spirit to have easier access to us.'[6]

When the supply of foreign medicines failed to be available to the opium refuge, Pastor Hsi of China faced a major challenge. It was absolutely vital to have medicine to continue appropriate treatment of patients. With no other course of action available, Pastor Hsi desperately sought the Lord with prayer and fasting, as to what he might do. As he continued to pray and fast the Lord instructed him on which ingredients could be used and in what proportions. Having written out a prescription and compounded the various medicines, he hastened back to his refuge to administer the new mixture. It succeeded so well that it entirely changed aspects of early opium refuge work.

Whatever principles are called into operation, the general testimony is that prayer is intensified, spirituality is sensitised and ministry is more powerfully effective.

Hallesby expresses a general sentiment when he says that:

> 'fasting helps to give us that inner sense of spiritual penetration by means of which we can discern clearly that for which the spirit of prayer would have us pray in exceptionally difficult circumstances.' [7]

Derek Prince tries to be more specific when he claims that:

> 'Fasting deals with two great barriers to the Holy Spirit ... self will ... and self gratifying appetites of the body (Galatians 5:19) ... With these carnal barriers removed the Holy Spirit can work unhindered in His fullness through our prayers ... Fasting makes way for the Holy Spirit's omnipotence.' [8]

Because of Prince's own personal experience, observations of others and interpretations of scriptures as to the meaning and effectiveness of prayer and fasting he concludes that:

> 'if God's people will go on to seek Him more earnestly with prayer and fasting on a wider scale, we shall see a move of the Holy Spirit throughout the entire world such as history has never yet recorded.' [9]

However that may be, in the practice of fasting, a caution needs to be added regarding personal attitudes. In Acts 13:2 it says, *'While they were worshipping the Lord and fasting ... '*. We need to remind ourselves that we do not fast out of self-centredness or for drawing attention to ourselves. It occurs within the context of worship and prayer 'unto the Lord'.

Jesus indicated that he was opposed to anything related to self-centredness with respect to prayer or fasting (Matthew 6:5–18). If we do it for selfish ends, forget it. It is not to be a means of getting something from God. It can never be reduced to formulas of exaggerated self denial.

Isaiah 58 is a classic chapter on fasting in the Old Testament. It teaches that fasting must be God initiated and God ordained. We are to be drawn by the Spirit, not dominated by the law (Galatians 5:18).

Fasting is not meant to impress others (Luke 18:12; Matthew 6:16–18). It is not a hunger strike to force God's hand to get our own way as politicians are wont to do (Jeremiah 14:10–12). It is not even meant to be a health kick. It is that which we do as a ministry unto the Lord.

For this reason God asked an earlier generation,

> '... *When you fasted ... was it really for me that you fasted?'*   (Zechariah 7:5)

Or was it self-initiated, self-ordained, self-promoted?

Whenever prayer and fasting are practised according to the ways and will of the Lord, then we may expect extraordinary responses from him.

When Waymon Rogers, pastor of Christian Life Centre in Louisville, Kentucky, led his people in round-the-clock praying, he saw their church grow from 200 to 2000. But when 200 people in the congregation began to fast every Thursday, the supernatural really broke through.

He reports:

> 'A woman with cancer was healed. God delivered people from demon possession. Many people were healed by the miraculous power of God. For four and a half months we had a revival where 10,000 people came each week to our church. They argued over who was going to get the front seats. People were saved and healed, and 4,600 people gave their hearts to God in that time. This was after the church had fasted and prayed for two years. The only problem we had was traffic jams ... Encourage your people to fast and pray!' [10]

In the light of evidence such as this, is it any wonder that Leonard Le Sourd concludes:

'Fasting is designed to make prayer mount up as on eagles' wings. It is intended to usher the suppliant into the audience chamber of the King and to drive back the oppressing powers of darkness, thereby loosening their hold on those being prayed for. Fasting definitely will give an edge to (a person's) intercession and power to ... petition.' [11]

Endnotes

1. Eastman, *Change the World School of Prayer*, 90.
2. Cho, *Prayer: Key to Revival*, 101.
3. Derek Prince, *Shaping History Through Prayer and Fastiny*. Fort Lauderdale, Florida: Derek Prince Ministries, 1973, 116.
4. Cho, *Prayer: Key to Revival*, 103.
5. *Every Home for Christ*, September 1993, 4.
6. Roland J. Hill, 'Fasting: A Discipline Ministers Need,' *Ministry*, March 1990, 6–8.
7. Oscar Hallesby, *Prayer*. London: Inter-Varsity Press, 1965, 117.
8. Prince, *Shaping History Through Prayer and Fasting*, 86–87.
9. *Ibid.*, 125.
10. Waymon Rogers, 'Fasting', *Church Growth*, December, 1988, 19.
11. Leonard Le Sourd, 'Does Fasting Increase Prayer Power'. *The Intercessors*, March, 1984.

Chapter 3

More Tough Stuff

Spiritual Warfare

In October 1993 church leaders in the city of Woolongong, Australia issued an urgent appeal to other churches around the nation. According to their bulletin, Satanists had gathered in their area from the United Kingdom, Canada, the United States and from within Australia for a month, to better establish the power of Satan emanating from that location. The satanic ceremonies were to climax on the weekend of the full moon October, 30–31.

The overt re-emergence in the West of witches' covens, satanic cults, widespread occult practices and Eastern religions has re-sensitised Christians to appreciate that the growth or decline of any church is a supernatural process. According to the sweep of biblical cosmology the church exists within a spiritually hostile environment. As a part of God's kingdom, its existence and growth is contested and inhibited by satanic forces. Individual believers are regarded as soldiers in this conflict (1 Timothy 1:18; 2 Timothy 2:3–4; Ephesians 6:11, 13). As such they may be adversely affected (Acts 14:22; 2 Timothy 1:5; 2 Timothy 3:10–12). Jesus taught that ways in which believers could overcome spiritual opposition include prayer and fasting (Matthew 17:21; Mark 9:29). Such conflict is referred to as *'spiritual warfare'* (2 Corinthians 10:3–5; Ephesians 6:10–18). Bringing people from darkness to light, from the power of Satan to that of God 'involves an inescapable element of (this) spiritual warfare'. [1]

David Shibley writes that 'while studies on methodology of evangelism are undoubtedly helpful good ideas don't produce harvest.' [2]

When asked for an explanation of how the Church on the Rock in Rockwall, Texas, which commenced only in January 1980, could have so rapidly grown to a point of receiving over four thousand people into membership by 1985, he replied:

'The evangelistic program of our church is the daily prayer meeting! For it is there at our daily prayer meeting that we bind the demon spirits that hinder the harvest, that we loose the Holy Spirit to draw the lost to Christ, that we beseech the Lord of the harvest to send forth labourers, and that we dispatch holy angels to do battle against the forces of Satan and bring people to Christ ... Each morning Monday through Friday we meet at 5.00 and 6.00 for prayer ...

If we see the harvest [of conversions] fall off for more than a week, we see that as a spiritual red alert and seek the Lord for more souls. When we cannot break through demonic resistance by normal means, we remember that Jesus taught that some demonic forces give way only by prayer and fasting (Matthew 17:21).

Again on Saturday evenings we meet to do nothing but pray for the harvest on the coming day. Also, the first Friday night of each month is given to an all-night prayer meeting. Again on Sunday morning ... [we] meet to pray one more time for the harvest. [3]

What concepts lie behind the practices which are so prominent and effective as factors in the unusual growth of that Church on the Rock?

The most fundamental concept is that there are two spiritual kingdoms – the kingdom of God and the kingdom of

Satan, or the kingdom of light and the kingdom of darkness (Colossians 1:13). Between these kingdoms war has been waged constantly.

Part of the reason for Jesus' incarnation was to reassert God's rulership, to liberate and claim back that which rightfully belonged to him. Part of his mission was to destroy the devil's works (1 John 3:8; Matthew 12:22–28).

While the defeat of Satan was achieved by Jesus's death and subsequent resurrection (Colossians 1:13–14; 2:14–15; Hebrews 2:14), Satan has not yet been destroyed. Satanic strongholds remain. Jesus has commissioned his disciples to participate in the mopping up operation (Acts 26:16–18). Toward that end appropriate warfare weapons are made available, for offensive and defensive purposes. These include:

Prayer and fasting (Matthew 17:21; Ephesians 6:18),
Truth (Ephesians 6:14),
Righteousness (Ephesians 6:14),
The Gospel (Ephesians 6:15),
Faith (Ephesians 6:16),
Salvation (Ephesians 6:17),
The Word of God (Ephesians 6:17),
The name of Jesus (Mark 16:17; John 14:14),
The blood of Jesus (Revelation 12:7,11).

Believers are expected to 'bind' demonic forces (Matthew 12:28–29; 18:18–20) and to 'loose' afflicted people from satanic bondages (Luke 13:16). Thus armed (Luke 10:19) and forewarned (Matthew 10:16; Romans 16:19–20; 2 Corinthians 2:11) believers are to engage the 'enemy'.

Satan, whose origins and development are somewhat obscure (Ezekiel 28:11–19; Isaiah 14:4–21; Luke 11:18), is regarded as the supreme enemy who is aided by other 'fallen' spirit beings (Luke 11:18; Jude 6; Matthew 25:41; 2 Peter 2:4), so that today

'our struggle is not against flesh and blood, but ... , against the spiritual forces of evil in heavenly realms.'
(Ephesians 6:12)

Some of these spiritual beings crave human habitation (Luke 11:24; Mark 9:17–18) or can occupy animals (Mark 5:12–13).

Paul seems to infer a differentiation of abilities or hierarchy of authority amongst Satan's allies when he refers to them as *'rulers, ... authorities, ... powers of this dark world,'* (Ephesians 6:13).

In the same verse he also ascribes location to them as *'spiritual forces of evil in heavenly realms'*, which may equate somewhat with the multiplicity of 'heavens' mentioned elsewhere in scriptures (Genesis 1:1; Psalm 148:4; 2 Corinthians 12:2–4; Ephesians 4:10).

Between spiritual 'location' and physical 'territory' there may be some connection. Daniel was appraised of malevolent spirit beings which ruled over Persia and Greece (Daniel 10:12, 20). That Daniel could receive the answer to his prayer was due only to the temporary assistance given to his unnamed messenger by the angelic prince, Michael (Daniel 10:13).

Similarly, satanic beings seemed to be the spiritual rulers over Tyre (Ezekiel 28:11–19), Babylon (Jeremiah 51:44; Revelation 17:3–5), Ekron (2 Kings 1:2–3), and the Abyss (Revelation 9:11).

Conversely, angelic beings were appointed to superintend the affairs of God's people in their locations (Revelation 2:1, 8, 12, 18; 3:1, 7, 14; Daniel 12:1).

On the concept of stationary spiritual rulership over physical domains, that is 'territoriality', one cannot be overly dogmatic as the biblical data is insufficient and inconclusive. This is in harmony with the tenor of scripture which seldom reveals too much of the specifics of demonic activity as if to discourage excessive human preoccupation with such which in turn could exalt Satan and diminish Jesus as the focus of our attention. On the one hand it should not be denied, while on the other it should not be focused on too much. [4]

What is more certain is that a cosmic spiritual battle climaxed at the cross (Colossians 2:13–15), troubles continue (Revelation chapters 12, 13, 17), sufficient authority has been delegated to believers to deal with these matters (Matthew 16:19; 28:19; Luke 10:19), and it is intended that believers be always victorious everywhere (2 Corinthians 2:14; Ephesians 2:4–6).

To ensure that outcome, they are to remain aware (2 Corinthians 2:11), alert (1 Peter 5:8) and active (Jude 20; 1 Peter 4:1), especially in the use of all spiritual armour (Ephesians 6:10–18) of which prayer and fasting are a part.

However, 'territoriality' as a concept is gaining ground, especially in the charismatic and pentecostal sections of the church where demonstrably also the most rapid rates of church growth are occurring. Peter Wagner is one of the better known popularisers of the concept.[5] He 'began by postulating that there were such things as very high level principalities and powers assigned in a satanic hierarchy to territories, people groups, cities, industries, governments and so on.'[6] As a church growth specialist, he was constrained to investigate further when he noted that the concept of territoriality was being actively pursued as a specialist practice within spiritual warfare, and that the outcome seemed to be significantly accelerated church growth in some South American locations, especially Argentina. Wagner expands the concept further in *Warfare Prayer*.[7]

For a previous generation, writers such as Jessie Penn-Lewis had similarly urged believers to engage in 'perpetual warfare in the Spirit ... against a spirit foe.'[8]

Floyd McClung's *Spirits of the City*,[9] John Dawson's *Taking our Cities for God*,[10] and George Otis Jr's *The Last of the Giants*,[11] are more popular contemporary expressions of the concepts.

To those who question the spiritual territoriality concept on the basis that it seems to have little precedent in Scripture, Wagner[12] replies that in that case, if we were to be totally consistent we ought not to refer to the Godhead as the 'Trinity'; there was no need to limit the Bible to sixty-six books; it is not necessary to worship on Sunday; there ought not to be church buildings, Christmas, Easter, Sunday schools, or even denominations as we know them could all disappear because none of the foregoing are specifically mentioned in Scripture either. Wagner, of course, is in no sense opposed to any of the above. But he makes the point that Christian beliefs and practice have traditionally emerged through reflection on experience married to what we know of the will of God revealed in the Word of God and principles embedded therein.

Paul did not have an instant developed Christology as a result of his Damascus road experience. That was merely the beginning of his inquiry (Acts 9:5). Obviously his theology developed from his personal and ministry experience. His interpretations and responses were hardly pre-empted by philosophical theological precedents like ours often are today, as if there was neither anything new to know nor experience. Paul was a task theologian. His understanding and practice developed from what he experienced literally 'on the road'. Wagner and other 'territorialists' are similarly goal oriented, discovering what 'works' and seeking to understand and explain God's works, in the light of God's word, in a reasonable and systematic way. That's a human response we call 'theology'.

Just as there is not biblical 'proof' for much of the church's practices or activities at Christmas or Easter yet there is biblical justification, because of a systematic collation of Christian concepts (as in the case of the Trinity) or God is glorified (as he was through the practice of emancipation of slaves). [13]

The kingdom of God has invaded the kingdom of Satan and is taking it by force (Matthew 11:11–12; 12:25–26). We as church and individuals are a part of the overcoming process (Matthew 16:13–19; Luke 11:20–22; Acts 1:8; Revelation chapters 2–3). Just as Paul had territorial encounters (Acts 13:6–12; 16:16–21) so we ought to anticipate spiritual warfare at three levels, ground (Acts 19:11–12), occult (Acts 19:18–20) and strategic (Acts 19:23–41). [14]

Certainly we seem to be learning more of the concept of spiritual territoriality through the practice of specialised evangelism and resultant church growth field experience than through specific, detailed biblical data. Dawson is right when he claims that 'ancient peoples were profoundly aware of territorial spirits.'[15] They still are.

In Australia, Christian Aborigines lament the fact that for decades western missionaries have remained disinterested and therefore ignorant of pagan Aboriginal worldviews in which spiritual territorialities are strongly embedded. The Aboriginal church also has remained small and weak. The rest of the nation is however, being forced to take notice. For the second time in 1991 a major industrial development was thwarted because of its alleged interference with the abode of 'Iltji', a local manifestation of the 'rainbow serpent'. Therefore at Yakabinie in Western Australia, A$10 million of development work and 100,000,000 tonnes of nickel and cobalt ore deposits remain undisturbed. Elsewhere, a similar fate has befallen gold and uranium reserves.[16]

It can never be more than speculation, but it is interesting to note that in the municipality of Nunawading in the city of Melbourne, Baptist, Uniting and Church of Christ denominations have all grown their largest congregations in Australia. Demographically, little separates this municipality from others in eastern Melbourne. However, Aborigines point out that this was the border area between major tribal groups which existed prior to European settlement and as such, presumably represents a location of less powerful spiritual hostility to Christianity than areas closer to the centres of tribal activities around Melbourne.

Robert Linthicum maintains that 'every city has a "spirit"'[17] and that each unit of society is protected and directed by its brooding angel.[18] 'If it is under the authority of God, its spirituality is "angelic", and if under Satan, "demonic".'[19]

To move from demonic domination to angelic direction and thus see an acceleration of church growth, what can be done?

In 1970 Jaques Ellul lamented how the devices of modern, western, secular, materialist society militated against a life of prayer.[20] R.A. Torrey described his generation (in 1924) similarly, but went on to issue this challenge:

'We live in a day characterised by the multiplication of man's machinery and the diminution of God's power. The great cry of our day is work, work, work, organise, organise, organise, give us some new society, tell us some new methods, devise some new machinery; but the great need of our day is prayer, more prayer and better prayer.'[21]

As God's church we may do many other things, but unless we pray, fast, and engage in 'spiritual warfare', it is unlikely that there will be any permanent change in a mostly moribund spiritual situation, at least in much of the western 'first' world. There may be significant church growth with prayer. There will probably be little without it.

Endnotes

1. 'Lausanne Committee Issues Statement on Spiritual Warfare,' *New Life*, October 1993, 10.
2. David Shibley, *Let's Pray in the Harvest*. Rockwall, Texas: Church on the Rock, 1985, 7.
3. *Ibid*, 7.
4. John Dawson, *Taking our Cities for God*. Milton Keynes, England: Word, 1989, 154.
5. C. Peter Wagner, *Wrestling with Dark Angels*. Eastbourne, England: Monarch Publications, 1990.
6. C. Peter Wagner, 'Hunting in the Heavenlies,' *On Being*, July 1991, 7.
7. C. Peter Wagner, *Warfare Prayer*. Tunbridge Wells, UK: Monarch, 1992.
8. Jessie Penn-Lewis, *Prayer and Evangelism*. Dorset, England: Overcomer Publications, n.d., 43.
9. Floyd McClung, *Spirits of the City*. Sussex, UK: Kingsway, 1990.
10. Dawson, *Taking our Cities for God*.

11. George Otis, Jr, *The Last of the Giants*. Tarrytown, New York: Chosen Books, Fleming H. Revell, 1991.

12. C. Peter Wagner, 'Strategic Level Spiritual Warfare: A Biblical Rationale', *Spiritual Issues and Church Growth Manual*, 1993.

13. *Ibid.*

14. *Ibid.*

15. Dawson, *Taking our Cities for God*, 156.

16. Duncan Graham, 'He Shall Not Be Moved,' *Good Weekend*, 16 November 1991, 68.

17. Robert C. Linthicum, *City of God City of Satan*. Grand Rapids, Michigan: Zondervan, 1991, 65.

18. *Ibid.*, 73.

19. *Ibid.*, 75.

20. Jaques Ellul, *Prayer and Modern Man*. New York: Seabury Press, 1970, 21–23.

21. R.A. Torrey, *The Power of Prayer*. Grand Rapids, Michigan: Zondervan, 1974, 190.

Chapter 4

So What Has Happened?

'By 3.15 a.m. the monks are already shuffling single file, like hooded bats in their billowing black robes, through the outside corridors of the monastery, their hands crossed on their chests as custom dictates, their bare feet cold on the wooden floors. For 30 minutes they chant sacred texts in the main hall, and then, in silence, eat a small breakfast, served from wooden containers, of gruel and pickled plums. Next, they file off to the 600 year old meditation hall, its screen open to the chilling dark, to concentrate on what is at the heart of their days and lives: Zen meditation. Nine figures sit perfectly erect in the pre-dawn blackness ... Immobile they remain as daylight comes to the bustling city of Kyoto.

In the bird scattered quiet of dusk, ... the monks return to meditation... At 9.00 p.m. they resume their silent sitting, outside in the cold ... Though some return before midnight to catch a few hours sleep on a tiny, body length tatami mat, others scarcely cease their meditation.'[1]

For the Buddhist, the purpose behind such extraordinarily disciplined, protracted meditation and prayer is to achieve detachment from all worldly entanglement, to achieve nirvana or enlightenment.

The Hindu also may engage in similarly Herculean feats

of self-discipline through prayer, fasting, and pilgrimage, preferably to break free from the endless cycles of reincarnation, or at least to ascend upward through the caste system in the next life.

One of the five 'pillars' of Islam also stresses the demands of daily prayer – five times per day in fact. The motive here is to fulfil another rigour of the Sharia or Law. If, for example, one of the daily prayer times is missed, then according to one Hadith or Tradition, the penalty is five thousand years in hell!

In each of these major religions, the purpose of prayer is fundamentally self-preservation for the future.

For Christians, the perspective of prayer is quite different. They are at peace with themselves, the present, and the future. It is assured by their acceptance of and submission to the Lordship of Jesus (John 1:12; 1 John 5:11–12). While their prayers may also be studded with legitimate gems of self-interest, their primary goal is to worship God and to seek his kingdom *'on earth as it is in heaven'*, (Matthew 6:9–10). In that God's kingdom exists in people, the prayers of God's people ought to include those for an increase in the number of people confessing Jesus Christ as Lord.

In Donald McGavran's seminal work, **Understanding Church Growth**, he identifies prayer as one of the major factors in accelerated, extraordinary church growth.[2] Martyn Lloyd-Jones agrees.[3]

Is this historically demonstrable? There is sufficient evidence from what we know of patterns of church growth over the last two centuries, to answer in the affirmative.

Extraordinary Church Growth 1790–1835

In the 1740s, John Erskine produced a pamphlet encouraging people to pray for Scotland. This publication in turn prompted Jonathan Edwards, in America, to produce what became a more influential document, *A Humble Attempt to Promote Explicit Agreement and Visible Union of God's*

***People in Extraordinary Prayer for the Revival of Religion
and the Advancement of Christ's Kingdom.*** [4]

Over the next forty years Erskine developed a network of
correspondents in the American colonies and European
states.

In 1781, as intercessors met at 3.00 a.m. in Cornwall on
Christmas day, the Holy Spirit 'fell'. Prayer increased and a
new movement was underway. By the mid-1780s in Northampton, Leicester, Bedford, Oxford, Yorkshire, Leeds, Shef-
field, and elsewhere, people were gathering in unprecedented
numbers to participate in what became known as 'Concerts
of Prayer'. These 'proved to be most significant, not only in
preparing the way for a general awakening but [also for]
preparing the way for the extraordinary outburst of missionary zeal in the last decade of the eighteenth century.' [5]

In England, awakening and growth there certainly was. It
commenced in the 1780s and exploded in the 1790s. In the
1790s Methodist membership quadrupled over what it had
been in the previous decade. Baptists and Congregationalists
were also reporting exponential growth. The number of 'dis-
senting' churches increased from 27 in 1739 to 900 by 1800,
5,000 by 1810, and 10,000 by 1820. Thomas Taylor, speaking at the annual Methodist conference at Leeds in 1797,
ascribed such growth to God's use of 'simple prayer meetings'. [6]

Becoming aware of what had happened in England, Christians in Wales and Scotland also organised special prayer
meetings for the same purposes with similarly encouraging
results.

Word spread across the Atlantic. New England ministers
banded together to issue a combined invitation to all believers of every denomination to join together in a concerted
effort to pray for revival. The first Tuesday in January 1795
was the suggested commencement date. [7] Methodists, Epis-
copalians, Congregationalists, Baptists, Reformed, and
others, responded fulsomely. In both northern and southern
states prayer and fasting among believers became the order
of the day.

What happened among Southern Methodists became typical. From a total membership of 4,753 in 1797 they increased to 53,648 by 1808, which represented an increase of approximately 40 percent per annum.[8] Orr considers that 'the Concert of Prayer begun in 1795 appeared to be the catalyst of action, the general intercession of God's people preceding an outpouring of the Spirit of God'.[9]

By 1815 in Britain and America, the call was renewed once more through the Concerts of Prayer for the need for further 'revival of religion'. Overcrowded prayer meetings and the practice of fasting again became commonplace. Those who responded positively reaped accordingly. For example, Primitive Methodists in the North Midlands of England numbered 7,842 members in 1820. By 1822 they had increased to 25,218.[10]

The 1830s saw an even more remarkable movement in America. As usual early morning and evening prayer meetings were its precedent.[11] Denominationally, growth among the General Conference of Methodists was fairly typical. In 1828 they had a combined membership of 418,927. By 1835 they had increased by 55.3 percent to 650,668.

The effects of the prayer movements were not confined to extraordinary growth in British and American churches. Apart from growth elsewhere in Europe, of greater long-term significance among Protestant churches was the resultant birth and growth of the cross-cultural missionary movement. William Carey, popularly regarded by many in the English-speaking world as the 'father of modern missions', was a member of a ministers' revival prayer group which had been meeting for two years (1784–86) in Northampton. In 1786 he shared his vision of God's desire to see the heathen won for the Lord.

What later became known as the Baptist Missionary Society was formed in 1793 after Carey had gone forth to Serampore in India on 30 May 1792. (The Australian Baptist Missionary Society commemorated the bicentennial event in 1992 by renewing the call for a prayer movement similar to that of which Carey was a part.)

Thomas Haweis proposed the formation of the London Missionary Society in 1795. The Scottish Missionary Society was founded in 1796 and three years later the (Anglican) Church Missionary Society was birthed.

Over in America, from the Concerts of Prayer movement came the New York Missionary Society in 1798.

From the 'haystack' prayer meeting came the first volunteers (for India in 1812) to go out with the newly formed American Board of Commissioners for Foreign Missions. The American Baptist Foreign Mission Society was formed in 1814. This was followed five years later by the Methodist Episcopal Church's own society.

> 'These missionary enterprises were sparked and driven by the Concert of Prayer in the sending countries, where awakened believers met regularly to pray for the revival of religion and the extension of Christ's kingdom. The first missionaries were all products of the revival.' [12]

In time, through prayer, discipline, and perseverance, they precipitated a new harvest in hitherto untouched fields.

Further Growth 1858–65

> 'The spiritual preparation for a world-wide awakening began in Britain seven years before the outpouring of the spirit there. Believers of one denomination after the other ... devoted the first Monday evening of each month to pray for a revival of religion and extension of Christ's kingdom overseas. This widespread union of prayer spread to the United States within ten years and to many other countries, and the Concert of Prayer remained the significant factor in the recurring revivals of religion and the extraordinary out-thrust of missions for a full fifty years, so common place it was taken for granted by the Churches.' [13]

Orr traces the beginnings of this period of accelerated

growth, at least in America, to an evangelistic crusade in Hamilton, Ontario which was conducted by Walter and Phoebe Palmer. [14] The media reported three to four hundred converts with similar results in subsequent meetings in Ontario and Quebec. South of the border this created a hunger for revival. In Pittsburg and Cincinnati, conventions established regular times for prayer and fasting. Baptist pastors in New York met for a whole day weekly to intercede for an outpouring of the Holy Spirit. Similar calls, meetings, and timetables were established amongst most other denominations.

Then a quiet businessman, Jeremiah Lanphier, who had been appointed by the Dutch Reformed Church as a missionary to the central business district of New York, called for a prayer meeting in the city to be held at noon each Wednesday. Its first meeting was 23 September 1857 and was eventually attended by just five other men. [15] Two weeks later it was decided to move to a daily schedule of prayer. Within six months, ten thousand men were gathering to pray. As the prayer movement spread throughout America it was accompanied by unprecedented, accelerated church growth. Church membership increased consistently by ten thousand persons per week during the next two years, giving an aggregate total of over one million new believers. Within a year, England, Scotland, Wales, and Ulster were being similarly affected.

As in the United Kingdom so also in America, the extraordinary visible growth of the churches had been preceded by some years of special prayer for such, prior to Lanphier's meetings. For example, a daily prayer meeting had been held in Boston for some years prior to 1858. Across Connecticut daily hour-long prayer meetings were held at 8.00 a.m. and 4.00 p.m., which might explain why later one town could report that there was not a single unconverted adult within their precincts. [16]

The first noon prayer meeting did not open in Philadelphia until 23 November 1857. Nothing much happened until March 1858 when suddenly six thousand people were in attendance. Mass conversions quickly followed. [17] In city after city the pattern was the same. Extraordinary massed prayer led to evangelism and massive results.

News of these events travelled and reached Ulster from Irish emigrants living in America. Sensing the same needs and opportunities in Northern Ireland, James McQuilkin and three other young men met for prayer in the Kells schoolhouse on 14 March 1859 to pray for revival. In May, a prayer movement was launched in Belfast. On 21 September, twenty thousand people assembled to pray for the whole of Ireland. It was later estimated that 100,000 converts resulted directly linked to these prayer movements. [18]

News of events in America and Ulster filtered through to Scotland, again with similar results. By 1859, the United Presbyterian Church was reporting on prayer meetings in Edinburgh, Glasgow, Aberdeen, and elsewhere. A quarter of its 162,305 members were praying for revival and church growth. [19] While definitive growth statistics are not available for Scotland, Presbyterian churches were reporting 10 percent growth rates for 1859. The following year would have hardly shown less. [20] It is thought that the total growth during this time in Scotland was at least 300,000. 'What had begun as an increase of prayer and intercession among the Christians became a great movement for the evangelisation of Scotland.' [21]

In Wales the pattern was repeated yet again. David Morgan (and others) at the village of Ysbytty Ystwyth had prayed for ten years for church renewal. Following news of the American happenings, special prayer meetings were called. In the period 1859–60 Congregationalists added 36,000 new members, Baptists 14,000, Wesleyans 4,549, and Presbyterians 36,190. The overall church growth for 1859–60 is estimated to have totalled 100,000. [22]

In 1859 Dr and Mrs Hamilton, who had been God's instruments in evangelism in Canada in 1857, visited Newcastle, England. Their visit had been preceded by twelve months of special prayer meetings interceding with God that he might do in England what he was doing elsewhere. Within a couple of months of the Hamiltons' visit, breakthroughs were occurring. Confirmed conversions increased to the thousands within the city.

By early January 1860, 'multitudes of believers' were united in various cities praying not just for England but for the whole world. [23] Within five years of that date churches in London alone had to increase seating capacity by 200,000. In England nonconformists gained at least 400,000 and the Church of England 250,000, giving a total estimated gain in 1859–60 in the United Kingdom of approximately 1,150,000. [24]

Patterns of missionary expansion were also similar to that which followed the revivals at the turn of the century. 'Thanks to the Revival in America and Britain, the work of established societies revived and new societies were formed in the 1860s.' [25]

Most notable was the foundation of what became known as the China Inland Mission by Hudson Taylor in 1865. He had received his vision and his mission's first candidates as products of prayer during the English revival. Taylor's mission presented a new model for subsequently formed interdenominational 'faith' missions. His move into inland China also encouraged similar moves into those provinces by the London Missionary Society, the American Board, Southern Baptists, the Church Missionary Society, and many others.

Micronesia, Indonesia, Algeria, Morocco, Tunis, Nyasaland, Malawi, Chile, Uruguay, Peru, Mexico, and Brazil were but some of the countries opened up by evangelical missions in the postprimary revival time. These new posts were staffed by converts of the revival who numbered among them such luminaries as Alexander McKay in Uganda and Mary Slessor in Calabar, West Africa. Kenneth Scott Latourette sums it up thus,

> 'Whatever the denomination, the large majority of the supporting constituencies and the missionaries were from those elements which had been affected by the Evangelical Awakening and kindred revivals.' [26]

Early Twentieth Century

Chronologically, the first growth burst appeared in Wales. Unlike its predecessors, there is little available evidence to suggest that this was preceded by protracted, organised, united prayer. There was intense prayer by its leaders, Evan Roberts and others. However, the public record at least only records this subsequent to the commencement of the revival in October 1904. Spontaneous, simultaneous lengthy prayer was a feature of many of the public meetings which in six months saw 100,000 people converted, 70,000 of whom came in the first two months. [27]

Events in Wales proved to be the ignition for extraordinary, accelerated growth patterns elsewhere. In January 1905, the General Assembly of Irish Presbyterians issued a call to prayer for a similar visitation of the Holy Spirit in Northern Ireland. A month later a call was also issued for the rest of Ireland. Quickly, twice-daily prayer meetings spread throughout the country. While the responses were not as numerous as those of five decades earlier, nevertheless many conversions and commissionings for ministry and missionary service were recorded. [28]

Simultaneously with events in Ireland, Scotland and England were also being affected. Mindful of the process of earlier revivals, leaders sent out calls for special prayer meetings. Nottingham, Gloucester, Bristol, Exeter, Devon, and Sussex, all started to report special prayer meetings with conversions quickly following. New Years' Day 1905, began with overcrowded prayer meetings in London and in at least two hundred other centres.

Those who promoted prayer and embraced the movement more strongly, reaped the greater harvest.

Among the greatest results were those of the Wesleyan Methodists in London. With a base membership of 54,785 persons, they added 50,021 in 1905 and 56,549 in 1906. [29] During the period 1903–8, Baptists increased by 18.9 percent (336,789 to 400,348) and Presbyterians by 12.3 percent (241,904 to 271,709). The pivotal year seemed to be 1900.

For example, while Baptists added 6,454 members in 1904, there was a 492 percent leap in annual additions to membership in 1905 (31,752 new members). [30]

In the mid-nineteenth century through revivals which commenced in America, expectations, the impetus to pray, and news of progress originally flowed from those who had emigrated to America from European countries, back to their countries of origin. In 1904–5 the process was reversed. In late 1904 news reached concentrations of Welsh immigrants in Pennsylvania of happenings back in Wales which encouraged them to pray, believe, and expect that a similar movement could occur in their land of adoption. By March 1905 the experiences of Wales were being repeated in Pennsylvania, with Methodists alone claiming ten thousand converts in Philadelphia. [31]

The pattern of calls to prayer, which resulted in a multiplicity of prayer meetings large and small, which was a part of the United Kingdom practice, was replicated in America. Noonday prayer meetings again became a feature of city life with business and government closing offices to accommodate the practice. Portland, Oregon, was typical. Over 'two hundred major stores signed an agreement to close between the hours of 11 a.m. and 2 p.m. to permit their customers and employees to attend prayer meetings.' [32]

Increases in membership during 1905–6 by various denominations across the country were reported as follows:

Increases in United States' Church Membership 1905–6

Year	1905	1906
Methodists	102,000	117,000
Baptists	72,667	93,152
Lutherans	51,580	116,087
Episcopalians	19,203	19,356
Presbyterians	18,803	48,006
Disciples	15,000	29,464
Total	279,253	423,065

Source: J. Edwin Orr, *The Flaming Tongue, The Impact of 20th Century Revivals* (Chicago: Moody Press, 1973), 86.

Although the effects of the accelerated growth flowed through quickly into the 1905 statistics, 1906, with a rise in the rate of the growth of new membership of 51.49 percent, was even more remarkable. [33]

However, by 1907 the growth spurt was tapering. In that year eleven major protestant denominations nationally grew by 5.4 percent. [34]

J. Edwin Orr in *The Flaming Tongue* goes on to tabulate the effects of what commenced in Wales, in other countries in the continents of Africa, Asia, Europe, and Australia. The pattern is usually quite similar. News of events in Wales triggered calls for intense, united prayer which were frequently followed by bursts of accelerated church growth during the subsequent two years. Obviously the pattern transcended location and culture.

As with previously similar spiritual movements, extension growth through missionary outreach was quite marked.

In Sweden almost one thousand school teachers formed a missionary organisation targeting Lapland, China, and South Africa. [35] It has been estimated that in America in 1896 two thousand candidates were involved in missionary training exercises. By the end of 1906 that number had surged to eleven thousand, with three hundred per year departing for cross-cultural ministries in foreign countries.

At the end of the first decade of the twentieth century, the World Missionary Conference in Edinburgh estimated that the first decade had experienced more church growth in Africa than at any other time in the history of the missionary enterprise. Protestants increased from 300,000 to 500,000 during 1903–10. [36]

Summarising western church growth during the period 1790–1907, Richard Lovelace concludes:

> 'Undoubtedly, the First Awakening increased the volume and quality of prayer among all participating. The Second Awakening was preceded in Britain by the "union of prayer" in which William Carey was active, and in the United States by the "concert of prayer"

promoted by Isaac Bachus. The 1857–58 Revival was phenomenally marked by prayer – whole denominations committed to prayer, the churches filled, and even theatres and public halls packed out at noon time. By prayer the movement spread in 1858–60 to the British countries. The Welsh Revival of 1904 arose and continued in prayer meetings ... History is silent about any great revivals that did not begin in prayer.'[37]

Endnotes

1. Pico Iyer. 'The Art of Life.' *Time*. 18 December 1989, 74.
2. Donald McGavran, *Understanding Church Growth*. Bombay: Eerdmans, 1970, 172.
3. Martyn Lloyd-Jones, *Revival*. Westchester, Illinois: Crossway Books, 1987, 161.
4. J. Edwin Orr, *The Eager Feet. Evangelical Awakenings 1790–1830*. Chicago: Moody Press, 1975, 14–15.
5. *Ibid.*, 17.
6. *Ibid.*, 19.
7. *Ibid.*, 53.
8. *Ibid.*, 69.
9. *Ibid.*, 78.
10. *Ibid.*, 97.
11. *Ibid.*, 139.
12. *Ibid.*, 126.
13. J. Edwin Orr, *The Fervent Prayer. The Worldwide Impact of the Great Awakening of 1858*. Chicago: Moody Press, 1974, xi.
14. *Ibid.*, 2.
15. *Ibid.*, 3–5.
16. J. Edwin Orr. *The Second Evangelical Awakening*. London: Marshall, Morgan and Scott, 1955, 25.
17. *Ibid.*, 29.
18. *Ibid.*, 41–46.
19. *Ibid.*, 48.
20. *Ibid.*, 83.
21. *Ibid.*, 53.
22. *Ibid.*, 56–59
23. *Ibid.*, 67.
24. *Ibid.*, 83.

25. Orr, *The Fervent Prayer*. 131.

26. Kenneth Scott Latourette. *A History of the Expansion of Christianity*, vol. VI, *The Great Century in Northern Africa and Asia (AD 1800–1914)*. London: Eyre and Spottiswoode, 1937–45, 336.

27. J. Edwin Orr, *The Flaming Tongue. The Impact of 20th Century Revivals*. Chicago: Moody Press, 1973, 17.

28. *Ibid.*, 32.

29. *Ibid.*, 48.

30. *Ibid.*, 47–48.

31. *Ibid.*, 70.

32. *Ibid.*, 80.

33. *Ibid.*, 86.

34. See raw data in Orr, *The Flaming Tongue*, 86.

35. *Ibid.*, 57.

36. *Ibid.*, 192.

37. Richard Lovelace, 'What Can We Learn From Past Spiritual Awakenings?' In *Unleashing the Power of Prayer*, ed. Vonette Bright and Ben A. Jennings, Chicago: Moody Press, 1989, 165.

Chapter 5

What About Today?

South Africa

Rees Howells was one who had been directly affected by the 1904 Welsh Revival. In particular, he had been most impressed by the fervency of prayer which accompanied that movement. He determined that more than anything else he would be an intercessor and encourage others to become likewise.

On 10 July 1915, he and his wife left England to join service with the South African General Mission. Fifteen months later, he was requested to undertake an extensive visitation of the mission's stations in what was then known as Swaziland, Pondoland, Bomvanaland, Tembuland, and Zululand. This tour was to last for two years. He prepared himself through intensive intercession and enlisted the help of others. The later assessment of the journey reads,

> 'The Holy Ghost came down on every station and gave revival, exactly as He had said He would do, and fulfilled the promise of the 10,000 souls.' [1]

Ethiopia

Later, during the Second World War, in part because of personal acquaintance with the Emperor of Ethiopia Haile

Selassie I, Howells and his co-prayers targeted Ethiopia for intercession. Because of the war, missionaries had been repatriated away from Ethiopia. When they returned at the conclusion of the Italian occupation, they found that in Walamo district alone the number of converts had increased from five hundred to twenty thousand. [2]

Ghana

Regarding elsewhere in Africa, Bright and Jennings refer to Ghana where 'prayer retreats, prayer seminars, all-night prayer meetings and Wednesday and Friday prayer and fasting meetings were intensified and resulted in revivals in churches,' which in turn produced evangelism, conversions, and numerical church growth. [3]

Australia

Australia has never experienced a national revival. Dr Stuart Piggin considers:

> 'The nearest [Australia has] come to a national revival was the 1959 Billy Graham Crusade, when a quarter of the population attended and 1.24 percent of the population accepted his invitation to accept Christ. There was a tremendous increase in church-going and many went into the ministry and to the mission field. The membership of Scripture Union doubled to 100,000. [4]

The 1959 Billy Graham meetings were preceded by a year of intense united prayer across all participating denominations.

While there has been no national revival, individual churches have discovered the link between prayer and church growth.

Senior Pastor Ron Frankland of Palm Beach Baptist Church in Queensland, in follow-up correspondence after the publication of a brief news item, [5] said that his church had had a deep commitment to prayer for some time. For over ten years the deacons met to pray at 6.00 a.m. every Sunday. More recently half nights and full nights of prayer were added as well as a bi-monthly Sunday 8.00–9.30 a.m. prayer slot. A visit from a group of Solomon Island pastors impacted the church further, to establish thrice weekly 4.00 a.m. prayer meetings. During the period 1969–79 the church grew from 70 to 230 members and is surging upwards once more.

At the same time, in personal correspondence, Pastor Gary Ninness of Margate Baptist Church in Queensland, reported that following a prayer seminar, the church was challenged to reconsider its commitment to corporate prayer. As a result, the church instituted quarterly prayer days (3.00 a.m.–7.00 a.m.), special half nights of prayer, and Wednesday evening prayer times. Within two years the church doubled its Sunday morning attendance from 50 to 100.

New Zealand

In New Zealand, George Pitt became the pastor of the North Island Birkdale Baptist Church's 20 members in 1978. By October 1984 the church had grown by 1,000 percent to 200 people, 50 others had been sent out to other Christian ministries, and six new churches had been planted. Pitt attributes his sense of mission, direction, success in evangelism, and church planting to a series of nine prayer and fasting sessions ranging from one to forty days' duration during this period. In an unpublished report Dr Bob Clinton also identifies 'prayer and fasting' as one of the major stimuli for the various kinds of growth in this church. [6]

Quinn Schipper, a pastor of Mairangi Bay Church of Christ Auckland, joined the church when it had declined to 49 members through losing 4 members per year over the preceding four years. Within twenty- two months it had bounced back to 77 members and was ministering to over 110 different people. In personal correspondence to C. Peter

Wagner on 2 December 1987, Schipper said that in his opinion the reversal from decline to growth was 'directly related
to commitment to and involvement in prayer to God.'

Papua New Guinea

Away to the north-west of New Zealand in Papua New
Guinea, the Enga Clans of the Western Highlands, with a
population in excess of 250,000, comprise the largest single
linguistic group in Papua New Guinea. They lived a totally
isolated existence until 1949 when American Lutheran,
German Roman Catholic, and Australian Baptist missionaries arrived in their midst. In the Australian Baptist area
amongst the Kyaka Enga of the Baiyer Valley area, the
church had grown to about two thousand members by 1961.
'By 1970 there was a general feeling of lethargy and even
despair throughout the Enga church.'[7] Several years previously, pastors from the Solomon Islands had visited the area
sharing with local leaders the blessings of revival which had
been in their churches for some time. From time to time
teams from the Solomons returned. 'Challenged by the low
state of local church life, and encouraged by the Solomon
Island stories of what it could become, many began to pray
for new life in the Enga church.'[8] Later, 'the prayer meetings
began with the Pastors and missionaries and among Bible
College students, but soon spread to the villages. In some
villages groups of people agreed to pray together every day
until God sent new life to the Church.'[9]

On Sunday 15 September 1973, without much prior indi-
cation, simultaneously in village after village as pastors
stood to deliver their normal Sunday morning messages the
Holy Spirit descended causing conviction, confession,
repentance, and revival. Normal work was stopped as
people in their thousands hurried to special meetings. Prayer
groups met daily morning and evening. 'Thousands of Christians were restored and thousands of pagans were converted
... Whole villages became 100 percent Christian ... and the
church grew not only in size but in maturity.'[10]

The Enga church has continued to grow quantitatively and qualitatively. Not only has it since sent out its own cross-cultural missionaries to evangelise the last few non-Christian tribes in Papua New Guinea, but it is also training missionary candidates for work in other countries including Australia!

A movement which commenced after people gave themselves to persistent prayer for about three years, not surprisingly, has been sustained by prayer. Most clans have built special 'prayer houses', separate and different from church buildings. Here family groups meet daily morning and night for Bible study and prayer.

Associated with these prayer places (*Loma panda*) are the Prayer Power Men (*Loma Pawa Akali*). These often were the 'Big Men' (*Numi*) who, prior to tribal conversion, led the clans. Because they were polygamous their leadership was forbidden in the church. They redirected their leadership abilities into politics and business which the church tended to regard as antithetical to Christian faith. Many of these genuinely revived natural leaders have their own special prayer places to which they retreat daily to intercede with God on behalf of their clans, and to listen for God's word on matters affecting their people. Commenting on the progress of the Enga church, experienced missionary Seaton Arndell notes that what has happened 'has come only in answer to prayer, because the church had come to the end of its resources and finally turned to God to plead for help.'[11]

Philippines

Within the same period, Bright and Jennings report that to the north of Papua New Guinea in the Philippines, following a visit to the International Prayer Assembly in Korea in the mid-1980s, two hundred missionaries of the Philippine Missionary Fellowship each organised a prayer group to meet daily at 7.00 p.m. to pray for the growth of the church in the Philippines. They report that directly from this activity there has since been established 110 new churches complete with their own buildings, and that there also is in existence a further 200 congregations who have yet to obtain buildings. [12]

China

Although the specifics remain unclear, one of the most amazing increases in church growth anywhere in the history of the church may have been going on for the last couple of decades in China. The most comprehensive report ever published on the church in China entitled *The Christian Occupation of China*, was issued in 1922. Most Christian bodies actively cooperated in its compilation.

The church was originally established within the precincts of the Treaty Ports bordering the south-eastern coast until progress was made inland. At the time of the declaration of the Peoples' Republic of China in October 1949, Christians were numbered between 700,000 to 1 million. In 1991 the estimate varied from a conservative twenty million [13] to fifty million. [14] But in June 1993, the State Statistic Bureau Report of the People's Republic of China officially declared that there were 63 million Protestant and 12 million Catholic Christians in China. [15]

While one cannot be too precise about numbers, what is certain is that there are vastly more Christians in China now than there were when the 'bamboo curtain' was lowered over four decades ago. In 1990 a high-ranking Communist official was reliably reported as complaining that in the central province of Henan alone the church had grown from 400,000 in 1982 to over 1 million by 1990. [16] One 'China-watcher', Tony Lambert, summarises his research by saying revival is spreading like wildfire. [17]

Although the church in China is still subject to information control, and therefore reconciling reports released inside China with those outside China has to be done with a great deal of care, no one any longer denies the existence of a vibrant growing body of mainland believers. What is of equal interest is that this phenomenon has occurred without outside assistance and, in fact, it is claimed that apart from prayer, no external help is needed. [18]

Several years ago, elderly Pastor Wang Mingdao explained:

'We have nothing – no pastors, no churches, no Bibles – nothing! We only have God. Therefore we go to Him in desperation.' [19]

David Wang concludes that the key to the phenomenal growth of the church in the Peoples Republic of China, is their fervent prayer. [20] Elsewhere he reports that through prayer, God 'is not their last resort. He is their first and only resort.' [21]

But to understand something of the current movement, it is necessary to examine foundations laid late last century and earlier in this one. The China Inland Mission (CIM), later renamed Overseas Missionary Fellowship (OMF), serves as an appropriate example.

In common with the founders of other major cross-cultural missionary societies, CIM was born as a vision through the persistent prayer of its founder, Hudson Taylor, on 25 June, 1868. [22] Having begun with prayer, Taylor so modelled intercessory importunity that within six months regular times were scheduled to pray in the first workers [23] and the funds to support them. [24] By 1881 he was encouraging groups of supporters to pray in an additional seventy new workers. [25] By 1887 the prayer request was increased to one hundred new workers for that year. [26] *'Ask the Lord of the harvest, ... to send out workers into his harvest field,'* (Matthew 9:38) was the practice Jesus had commended. Taylor did just that and his national and foreign staff were consistently provided and provided for.

For Taylor, prayer was the key to the provision of labourers and for planting the church. When Jonothan Goforth was preparing to leave Cheffoo for Pangchwang, Taylor advised, 'Brother, if you would enter that Province, you must go forward on your knees.' Goforth adopted the challenge so that Taylor's advice became the 'slogan' for the North Honan Mission.[27] Goforth also considered that prayer was one of the critical factors in Finney's 'appropriate means'[28] for reaping great spiritual harvests, resulting in many new churches. Goforth made a lifelong priority of prayer and participated in revivals in China and Korea.

Early in this century CIM missionary, James O. Fraser, was impressed by the amount of time Taylor's replacement, D.E. Hoste allotted to prayer.[29] He therefore determined that the priority of his life would be similar. 'To know the real Fraser one needed to hear him in prayer. Prayer was the very breath of life to him, and in prayer he seemed to slip from time into eternity.'[30] He determined prayer would have first, second and third place in his life.[31] Fraser's target people were the Lisu tribes of Yunan province bordering on Burma. 'Solid lasting missionary work is done on our knees. What I covet more than anything else is earnest believing prayer,' was his message to his co-intercessors for the Lisu.[32]

On 12 January 1913, having been on the field for three years, Fraser first prayed specifically for 'several hundreds of families' to become Christian among the Lisu. This was the unswerving prayer goal which he shared with his prayer partners on 9 October 1915.[33] Suddenly, without warning, seven years later in 1922 on what could have been his last journey among the Lisu, 'Family after family, ... village after village' started to make public decisions to become Christian. Quickly 5–600 people representing approximately 3,000 people formed the new 'instant' church.[34] Fraser saw this breakthrough as a result of the 'spiritual warfare' his intercessors had been waging on behalf of the Lisu in terms of Ephesians 6:12.[35]

J. Edwin Orr documents prayer movements in China in the first decade of the twentieth century.[36] These were followed by a 57 percent increase in Chinese communicants from 113,900 to 178,000 up to 1906. At the annual CIM meeting in Melbourne, Australia in 1915, A.G. Nicholls shared relevant information on how some of this church growth occurred. He claimed that in 1904, 15,000 Miao from 350 villages turned to God. By way of explanation of the phenomenon he added,

> 'Practically no preparatory work had been done amongst the Miao. In answer to the earnest and persistent prayers of God's people, the Lord opened the door and we missionaries went in to reap harvests of golden grain.'[37]

Other reports are available of the work and results of other missions. It is suggested that only against this background can some understanding of the current growth phenomena of the Chinese church be understood. From the beginning it was a church birthed by trial, adversity, perseverance, and prayer – much more so than is common in contemporary western experience.

While detailed evidence of church growth in China during the last four decades is patchy, the church has certainly not died as some western scholars assumed it would. In fact the reverse is the case.

In the provinces of Fujian and Zhejiang, official statistics list 700,000 Christians in Zhejiang and 600,000 in Fujian.[38] In Dengfeng county of Henan province, the number of Christians grew from a handful in 1949 to 30,000 by 1986. In Northern Anhue in the town of Huoqiu, one small church and two outstations planted by the CIM, from 1949 to the mid-1980s had increased to a regular congregation of 3–4,000 and about 200 house churches meeting in the same county.

In 1947 Christians numbered 2–300 only among the Yi. All church work was closed down in 1952. However, by 1991 in one county there were 6,000 mainly Yi Christians, and 30,000 in nearly 300 churches in adjacent Luquan County.[39]

In 1949 the number of Christians in Inner Mongolia were few. By 1990 their number was estimated at 1.5 million.[40] When the official number of Christians was only 700,000 in

1949, these current official statistics are indeed impressive. Growth continues unabated, especially so since the Tiananmen Square massacre. 'A recent Communist Party report stated that whereas applications for Party membership had declined drastically, converts in Christian churches had doubled, tripled or quadrupled in many major cities.'[41]

In trying to identify causes for such explosive growth, David Wang lists faith, fellowship, radical obedience to the Word of God, and (true to their founding traditions) fervency in prayer.[42] Having for so long been deprived of Bibles and hymn books, it is common for corporate prayer in services to go on for some hours. Fasting is also an integral part of their prayer life.[43] Individuals give over much of their early morning hours to prayer and private devotions.[44]

But one suspects it is not only prayer from within China that has contributed to such rapid growth. An important component exists outside China. Since the expulsion of the last of the foreign missionaries in 1951, exiled missionaries and their societies, overseas Chinese and many others have been relentless in their prayer for China.[45]

'Hudson Taylor early learned the priority of prayer in his life. The Church in China was born in prayer. So in the time of her greatest need prayer became the bulwark of the persecuted Church ... No Westerner can equal the ardour of the praying saints of China.'[46]

In such an environment the story of the Xiao may be repeated many times over.

In 1987, an American Mission Board appointed a 'non-residential' missionary to focus on the sixteen million Xiao, who were among the least evangelised people in the world. For the Xiao there were no residential missionaries, no Christian institutions, and no Bible or hymn book. By 1988, however, over five hundred churches, as well as tens of thousands of others doing likewise around the world, were committed to pray for these people. Tentmaker missionaries were able to move into the area and by 1988 there were also

3 converts. In 1989 that number had risen to 3,000. By mid-1990 it had leapt to 30,000! The authors of the report on the Xiao attribute the growth primarily to the fact that these people are the prayer focus of so many churches and people. [47]

Who can accurately calculate the positive effects of such a volume of prayer rising up as incense (Revelation 5:8)?

In the West we are starting to understand the negative effects of the lack of such prayer. In the United States of America, Scholastic Aptitude Tests plummeted, divorce rates, the incidence of violent crime, and the number of high school dropouts suddenly increased in 1963. One year before, in 1962, the United States Supreme Court (Engel v. Vitale) ruled that prayer be banned from public schools. With the value of approximately thirty years hindsight, we can develop almost perfect vision and postulate that 'a strong correlation exists between the exclusion of God from public affairs and the break-up of our families', [48] and other deleterious social and national effects.

In China, the church grows rapidly stronger while in the West it grows weaker. Perhaps it is because we prefer to organise rather than match the zeal of the praying saints of China.

'Outside of China, the Church emphasises organisation. Inside China, the Church emphasises direction – the direction of the Holy Spirit.' [49]

Dr James Hudson Taylor III, a great grandson of Hudson Taylor and General Director of Overseas Missionary Fellowship, likens China's Christians to believers in the book of Acts. They were known as 'those who call on the name of the Lord'. They were a people of prayer. Dr Taylor asks,

'I wonder if we (the Christians of the free world) would be described as such? Or have we lost something of that life of prayer?' [50]

Korea

A far more reliably documented example of national church growth is China's northern neighbour, Korea.

Missionary work started in Korea in the last decade of the nineteenth century. The first signs of extraordinary church growth occurred in what is now North Korea, in the city of Pyongyang. In 1905 in the space of two weeks there were 700 converts. In 1906, in the district of Pyongyang the number of Christians rose to 6,507, while in the following year of 1907 there was also about 45,000 converts elsewhere in the country. By 1912 Korean church members totalled 300,000. [51]

The most remarkable aspect of Korean church growth is that its high rate has been maintained for several decades. If it continues, it is estimated that by the end of this decade more than 50 percent of the nation will be Christian. Today in Korea there exist the world's largest Pentecostal, Methodist, Presbyterian, and other denominational churches. The largest of these is Yoido Full Gospel Central Church in Seoul, South Korea. By 1988 their membership was 750,000 and they were seeing 10–12,000 converts per month.

What is it that has made the growth of the Korean church so distinct from all others in this century? Regardless of whatever conclusions other analysts may reach, the Koreans' answer in one word is 'prayer'. Peter Wagner is 'convinced that Korea's greatest gift to contemporary Christianity is prayer.' [52]

Donald McGavran was of the opinion that 'prayer [is] what God wants His people to offer'. [53] That is certainly what is being offered in Korea. Paul Yonggi Cho, the country's most widely known pastor, understands that no revival has ever occurred 'without people realising that they must pray ... long concentrated prayer'. [54] He is also aware that the early morning prayer meetings formed 'one of the most important aspects of the early [Korean] church', [55] and like most other pastors he has been careful to maintain the practice, thereby prolonging revival. [56] In fact, it is normal for church members in Korea to gather daily from 4.00 a.m. onwards for united prayer. Prayer meetings are usually held also throughout the night each Friday.

Many churches own prayer retreats known as 'prayer mountains'. Cho frequently asserts that any church which is prepared to 'pray the price' and to 'pray and obey' may see results similar to those which are commonplace in Korea. Because of the atmosphere of prayer, Cho finds it easier to preach in Korea and audiences are more responsive there than elsewhere. [57]

However else church growth analysts may choose to explain the Korean protracted church growth, local believers have little doubt that it is due to the preeminence of prayer and fasting. Cho expresses it thus:

> 'You could remove the powerful preaching from our church and it would still continue. You could remove the administration of pastoral care through the cell group system and the church would still continue. But if you removed the prayer life of our church it would collapse.' [58]

For Korea, prayer is the declared primary factor in their sustained growth throughout the twentieth century. In that no other country anywhere near matches their growth rate, even without any biblical base, the probability of their being correct would remain quite high. We must listen to the Korean church.

In answer to the question of 'Why the Korean church has flourished so magnificently in the last 50 years', a Korean pastor replied

> '... We learned to have no hope in ourselves, but only in God. And we learned to pray. We have been a suffering church and, therefore, a praying church.' [59]

Argentina

A final 'hot spot' of unusually sustained church growth which needs noting is Argentina.

The census of 15 May 1991, provisionally reckoned Argentina's population to be 32.4 million. It is constitutionally declared a Roman Catholic country, and has proved to be consistently one of the least responsive countries in South America to gospel preaching. In 1983, evangelicals were 1 percent of the population, but by 1988 were estimated to number between 1.5 million and 3 million (4.7 percent and 9.4 percent). Whichever figure is correct, the growth is impressive. Some of this growth is typified in what are becoming internationally known churches.

Hector Gimenez started The Miracles of Jesus Renewed Christian Church in 1983. The congregation numbered 70,000 in 1992.

Omar Cabrera's The Vision of the Future Church started in 1972 with 15 members. At the end of a year there were 140 members. By the end of the third year, after 540 consecutive nights of preaching, it was 4000 strong. Its membership in 1992 was 90,000 in 121 cities.

La Plata Evangelical Pentecostal Church (AOG), of which Alberto Scataglini is pastor, was 500 strong in 1983. By 1991 it had grown to 2,500.

Peter Wagner rightly poses the question, 'What is the secret behind such effective ministry?'[60] While he rightly cautions against oversimplification because of the complexity of factors involved in church growth, he ultimately concludes that the primary distinctive in Argentinian church growth is their willingness to engage in spiritual warfare. 'Powerful intercessory prayer is [the] chief weapon.'[61]

Carlos Annacondia is one of the better known 'warriors'. He is an evangelist who, like others, secures broad denominational support, preaches lively messages, makes appeals and uses trained counsellors. But unlike other (western) evangelists, he engages in 'intentional premeditated, high energy ... spiritual warfare'.[62] Deliverance specialists work in a large marquee on the crusade site nightly from 8.00 p.m. to 4.00 a.m. Not only are the results of such crusades remarkable, but what happens in the cities after an Annacondia crusade is even more significant. Jose Luis Vasquez saw his church explode from 600 to 4,500, with a constituency of 10,000 in the five years following Annacondia's visit. [63]

Edgardo Silvoso heads up Harvest Evangelism Inc. They have had a three-year programme for evangelising the city of Resistencia. 'The great response we have seen to the proclamation of the gospel in Resistencia has to do almost exclusively with the teaching and implementing of spiritual warfare principles,' Silvoso says. He claims that traditional preaching is like standing outside a prison and telling the inmates how good freedom is. Hearers have been blinded and bound and need releasing (2 Corinthians 4:3–4; Acts 26:18). [64] Through discernment, Silvoso and his team claim to gain a knowledge of which spirits hold sway over a city. They then bind and banish such influences as a practice of pre-evangelism. To assist the process, other members of the team develop a spiritual map of a given area [65] to plot and counteract areas of demonic concentration. [66]

Omar Cabrera operates similarly. Before preaching in any new location he fasts and prays (up to forty days) to discern and disarm spiritual enemy strongholds. Aggressive, specific, spiritual warfare type praying is becoming commonplace in the fabric of South American evangelism, which is contributing so much to the area's church growth.

Las Acacias Evangelical Pentecostal Church in Caracas, Venezuela, has grown from 500 to 3,000 in the last decade. For sixteen hours a day, 5.00 a.m. to 9.00 p.m., people are praying in its sanctuary. Its pastor Samuel Olson attributes prayer as the major factor for the church's growth. He says, 'If you took away our prayer ministry our growth would cease and sputter out.' [67]

The most widespread international phenomenon of church growth this century has been the rise of the Pentecostal movement. They and others have thought that such unprecedented growth might be attributable to such factors as the distinctiveness of their theology, their lively contemporary style of services, signs and wonders, and their apprenticeship models of training. But a simpler reason for such growth may be far less complex and more fundamental – namely, that they pray and pray more than others. Walter Hollenweger is closest to the mark when he notes that 'from the earliest Pentecostals onward it was more important to pray than to organise'.[68] Although all Christians would probably acknowledge the necessity of prayer for church growth, it may be the Pentecostals who today depend most upon this channel of power.[69]

However, as has also been seen, from a study of growth patterns beyond the rise of modern Pentecostalism, the link between prayer and church growth is certainly not confined to that movement. In the English-speaking world alone, examples abound outside of revival movements[70] to demonstrate that more than theology, style, physical resources, and suchlike, prayer may still be the preliminary, primary, dominant factor.

Endnotes

1. Norman Grubb, *Rees Howells Intercessor*. London: Lutterworth Press, 1952, 166.
2. *Ibid.*, 223.
3. Vonette Bright and Ben A. Jennings, *Unleashing the Power of Prayer*. Chicago: Moody Press, 1989, 21.
4. Stuart Piggin, 'Revivals Common in Australia,' *The Victorian Baptist Witness*, August 1991, 17.
5. 'Palm Beach Proves Power of Prayer,' *The Queensland Baptist*, November 1989, 7.
6. Bob Clinton, 'Fasting, Prayer and Church Growth,' TMs, n.d., Original in the hand of author, Melbourne, 14.
7. R. Seaton Arndell, 'The Revival Among the Kyaka Enga People of Papua New Guinea,' Tms, n.d., Original in the hand of author, Sydney, 3.
8. R. Seaton Arndell, 'Revival in the Enga Church,' Tms, 1973, Original in the hand of author, Sydney, 4.

9. R. Seaton Arndell, 'Revival and Mission,' *The Australian Baptist, May 1990, 16.*

10. *Ibid.*, 46.

11. *Ibid.*, 47.

12. Bright and Jennings, *Unleashing the Power of Prayer*, 22.

13. Tony Lambert, 'China Crisis,' *Alpha*, August 1991, 20.

14. David Wang, *And They Continued Steadfastly.* Hong Kong: Asian Outreach International Ltd, n.d., 1.

15. Charles W. Spicer Jr., 'It's True! High Estimates of Christian Converts in China Confirmed,' *Overseas Council Newsletter*, October 1993, 3.

16. Lambert, 'China Crisis,' 20.

17. *Ibid.*, 20.

18. Richard Van Houton, 'The State of the Church in China,' Tms, 1984, Original in the hand of author, Hong Kong, 5.

19. David Wang, 'And They Continued Steadfastly. Part I,' *Asian Report*, July/August 1993, 22.

20. David Wang, 'And They Continued Steadfastly. Part II,' *Asian Report*, September/October 1993, 20.

21. *Ibid.*, 22.

22. Marshall Broomhall, *The Jubilee Story of the China Inland Mission.* London: Morgan and Scott Ltd, 1915, 24–25.

23. *Ibid.*, 35.

24. *Ibid.*, 36.

25. *Ibid.*, 156.

26. *Ibid.*, 172–73.

27. Rosalind Goforth, *Jonothan Goforth.* Minneapolis, Minnesota: Bethany House, 1986, 45.

28. *Ibid.*, 100–101.

29. Eileen Crossman, *Mountain Rain.* Singapore: Overseas Missionary Fellowship, 1982, 127.

30. Mrs O.J. Fraser and Mrs Howard Taylor, *Fraser and Prayer.* London: China Inland Mission, 1963, 5.

31. Crossman, *Mountain Rain*, 188.

32. Fraser and Taylor, *Fraser and Prayer*, 26.

33. Mrs Howard Taylor, *Behind the Ranges Fraser of Lisuland South West China.* London: OMF, 1944, 107–17.

34. Fraser and Taylor, *Fraser and Prayer*, 44–45.

35. Taylor, *Behind the Ranges*, 228.

36. J. Edwin Orr, *The Flaming Tongue, 158–60.*

37. A.G. Nicholls, 'How God is Working Among the Tribes,' *China's Millions*, January 1919, 4.

38. Tony Lambert, 'Patterns of Growth and Continuity: The Historical Context.' Uncompleted MPhil diss., 1991, 11.

39. *Ibid.*, 11–14.

40. Loren Cunningham, 'The Caleb Report,' *Ministries Today*, January/February 1990, 62.

41. Tony Lambert, 'Return to Tiananmen – One Year After,' *The Queensland Baptist*, August 1990, 8.

42. David Y.P. Wang, *Eight Lessons We Can Learn From the Church in China*. Hong Kong: Asian Outreach International, n.d., 10–14.

43. Wang, *And They Continued Steadfastly*, 15.

44. Eric E. Wiggin, 'The Church Since Chairman Mao,' *Moody Monthly*, October 1988, 85.

45. Sylvia Houliston, 'Did The Atheists Win.' In *When People Pray*. Singapore: Overseas Missionary Society, 1987, 94.

46. *Ibid.*, 96.

47. David V. Garrison, *The Nonresidential Missionary*. New Hope, Alabama: Missions Advanced Research Centre, 1990, 65–66.

48. David Barton, 'Did School Prayer Work?' *Ministries Today*, May/June 1991, 97.

49. Wang, 'And They Continued Steadfastly. Part II', 21.

50. *Ibid*, 23.

51. Orr, *The Flaming Tongue*, 166–69.

52. David Bryant, *Concerts of Prayer*. California: Regal Books, 1984, 48.

53. McGavran, *Understanding Church Growth*, 166.

54. Paul Y. Cho and R. Whitney Manzano, *More Than Numbers*. Gwent, UK: Valley Books, 1983, 104.

55. Paul Y. Cho, *Prayer: Key to Revival*. Waco, Texas, Word, 1984, 12.

56. *Ibid.*, 17.

57. *Ibid.*, 22.

58. Jim Williams, 'Seoul Secrets,' *Church Growth*, June 1989, 8.

59. Kenneth S. Kartzer, 'What Happens When Koreans Pray,' *Christianity Today*, August 1993, 13.

60. C. Peter Wagner, 'Spiritual Power in Urban Evangelism: Dynamic Lessons from Argentina,' *Evangelical Missions Quarterly*, 27, April 1991: 132.

61. *Ibid.*, 132.
62. *Ibid.*, 135.
63. C. Peter Wagner, 'Argentina's Annacondia,' *Ministries Today*, September/October 1990, 36.
64. Ed Silvoso, 'The Principle Behind the Strategy,' *Harvest Now*, September/October 1990, 4.
65. The spiritual mapping concept is further developed by George Otis, Jr, *The Last of the Giants*. Tarrytown, New York: Chosen Books, Fleming H. Revell, 1991, 84–102.
66. Rod Denton, 'Argentina, The Land of the Awakened Church.' Unpublished MA research paper, Fuller, Pasadena, 1991, 26.
67. C. Peter Wagner, 'Praying and Growing,' *Ministries Today*, May/June 1990, 56.
68. Walter J. Hollenweger, *The Pentecostals*. Minneapolis, Minnesota: Augsburg, 1972, 29.
69. Elmer L. Towns, John N. Vaughan and David J. Seifert, *The Complete Book of Church Growth*. Wheaton, Illinois: Tyndale, 1981, 193.
70. Brian Mills, *Three Plus Three Equals Twelve*. Eastbourne: Kingsway, 1986, 165–66.

Chapter 6

Where the Rubber Hits the Road –
A Strategy

During 20–25 August 1985, Rod Denton who was then an associate pastor of Blackburn Baptist Church in Melbourne, Australia, attended the sixth Church Growth International Conference held at Yoido Full Gospel Church in Seoul, Korea. There were thirteen hundred delegates from twenty-six nations. In a report back to his church, Pastor Denton identified four key characteristics of the Yoido church. In order of importance he listed them as:

1. Prayer
2. Preaching
3. Cell groups
4. Organisation and administration.

In the report's concluding seven recommendations, not surprisingly, his first recommendation was that:

> 'The church needs to establish a high priority on prayer. Pastors and leaders need to be men and women of prayer. Prayer needs to be taken seriously in cell groups and emphasis on church prayer meetings needs to be much higher. Through prayer, we need to understand that Satan's stronghold on our community can be broken and revival can occur.' [1]

However, such prayer ministries as Yoido Full Gospel Church exhibit don't just happen. Organisation and administration are also a vital part of the process of establishing, growing, and maintaining any ministry. Churches in the western world in particular are usually well organised. Sunday schools, women's and youth work, property and finance departments – everything, it seems, has its own paid or honorary co-ordinator, administrator, executive committee, or such like, to ensure that the relevant department functions according to policy guidelines, meeting goals, reporting to the next higher level of authority, or whatever is required of it.

However, when it comes to the church's prayer life, this is usually left to chance, [2] inspiration, the ladies' missionary support group, the pastor, or someone else. It is usually the 'other person's' responsibility to attend and nobody's responsibility to organise and monitor. Hence, it is not surprising that 'the fact of the matter is that contemporary prayer meetings often do not attract even some of the most likely candidates for leadership.' [3]

Although pastors need to delegate more than they usually do, one of the reasons for the state of corporate prayerlessness in many churches is the pastor's unwillingness or inability to do something about it. Mark Buckley, senior pastor of Living Streams Christian Church in Phoenix, Arizona, puts his finger on a part of the problem when he confesses, 'I tend to avoid planning and organisational meetings whenever possible because they bore me. I'd rather be out ministering to people than doing church administration.' [4] His attitude is typical of strongly gifted, people-oriented pastors who prefer relational to task orientation. Fortunately, through his observation of the Gulf War in 1991, he learned the value of strategic planning and that nothing much of sustainable value happens without it.

There are at least seven keys to unlocking a church's prayer potential and to seeing this unleashed power harnessed and directed toward the growth of the church. These are:

1. Motivation
2. Inspiration
3. Information
4. Communication
5. Location
6. Implementation
7. Evaluation.

Motivation

The title of Jonathan Edwards's still famous tract calling people to prayer commenced with the words, 'A humble attempt to promote...' Edwards 'understood that promotion was biblical. Like sounding the Levitical trumpet in the Old Testament, promotion is not to create the prayer movement, but to call people into it. A prayer movement needs motivated people.'[5]

The question is, How may they be motivated?

1. By the prospect of obtaining knowledge of God

From time immemorial people intuitively have yearned for a deeper knowledge of God. In the Bible from Moses (Exodus 33:13) to Paul (Philippians 3:10) this desire has been articulated. Paul's express wish was to know the Lord more intimately, progressively, continuously, heart to heart, and mind to mind. The force of the word and tense of the verb he uses for 'knowing' in Philippians 3:10 is not dissimilar to that of the Hebrew, when it says Adam 'knew' his wife Eve (Genesis 4:1, 25).

Not only was this Paul's desire for himself, it was his constant prayer for other believers (Ephesians 1:17; Colossians 1:10). This intimacy is only developed through the communion of prayer.

2. By accepting we are co-partners

That God accepts and elevates us to co-worker status (2 Corinthians 6:1) is heady stuff which should attract the shallowest thinker toward a desire to know God better. We are not just ordinary co-workers, there is also a touch of royalty about us (1 Peter 2:5)!

3. By becoming ambassadors

Not only are we exalted to the position of co-worker, we are sent forth into foreign, hostile, (spiritual) territory as God's ambassadors (2 Corinthians 5:20), with him choosing to make his appeal through us. Therefore, it is incumbent upon us again both to get to know whom we represent and what are the instructions he wishes us to convey or carry out (1 John 2:3).

4. By experiencing God's love

As we continue to obey him we enter into reciprocated, undeserved, love (Romans 5:8; John 13:34–35; 2 John 6; 1 John 4:8) which fills us with peace, joy and hope (Romans 5:1–3), and which makes us fearless (1 John 4:18).

5. By seeing as Jesus sees

As by inward renewal (2 Corinthians 5:17) and association we become more conformed into the likeness of Jesus (Romans 8:29), we start to be sensitised to people's needs and begin to sense and see the way Jesus sees (Matthew 9:36–37). The embarrassment and self-condemnation of our own blindness and insensitivity are removed as we follow through to be inspired to ask him for more harvest co-workers and see him answer (Matthew 9:38) by increasing harvesters and harvest.

6. By asking and then receiving

There is no problem with asking God for something provided our motives are correct (James 4:2–3). In fact, we are positively encouraged to ask (John 14:14; 16:24; Matthew 7:7). Providing we believe (Matthew 21:22), ask according to his will (1 John 5:14), and remain obedient (John 15:7), we know that we have been heard and the answer is on the way. While prayer to the Almighty is hardly to be compared with children wandering with a free wish list in a toy shop, yet a potent stimulus to continue to pray is the knowledge that he does reward those who earnestly seek him (Hebrews 11:6).

7. *By knowing there is yet more*

God wants to do more in and through us than that for which we can even imagine and ask (Ephesians 3:20). Thus it is not a matter of how much he can do, but what are the limitations of our sanctified imagination. In terms of church growth potential, given that God is *'not wanting anyone to perish, but everyone to come to repentance'* (2 Peter 3:9), not even 'the sky is the limit'. It is beyond our imagining.

8. *By hastening ultimate victory*

According to Ephesians 6:11–12, we are involved in constant spiritual warfare (whether we are aware of it or not). Prayer is the major offensive weapon we use to overcome spiritual enemies (Ephesians 6:18). Again, to know that we are on a side which cannot lose ought to be considerable impetus to participate. The church is not crouched down behind ramparts in a last-ditch defence against onrushing satanic hoards. The imagery in the scripture is the reverse. The church is on the offensive and its opposition has taken up defensive, self-protective positions behind ramparts which cannot withstand its relentless attack. The gates of an ancient city were always the most fortified, fiercely defended location in the whole of the perimeter of any fortress. Not even those (of hell) can stand against the church militant (Matthew 16:18). 'If God's people would only accept their sacred role as the army of God, ... if they would join in ... intercession ... we could see the greatest harvest of souls we have ever known.' [6]

With some of these untapped resources and unexperienced realities as powerful motivators toward prayer, is it any wonder that Paul, whose knowledge of God and experience in his work was way beyond our average, encourages us to be praying *'on all occasions with all kinds of prayers and requests'*, and to *'be alert and always keep on praying'* (Ephesians 5:18)?

In addition to the above, B.J. Willhite sees some other powerful motivators to pray. He says that:

1. If people understand that their own prayer really does make a difference (Joshua 10:8–13; Ezekiel 36:37);
2. If they understand that God has chosen to do nothing without them;
3. If people know how to deal with their doubt (Acts 12:1–17), and
4. If they really can believe God (Hebrews 11:6)

then they really will start to pray. [7]

In addition to all of the above, people in many churches have perhaps an additional even stronger motive to pray for church growth. For their churches it could be in the medium term, a life-and-death matter.

Dean Drayton, having studied many churches on the Australian scene, concluded that 'many are caught in a death cycle which will see them decline and die within fifty years of being established.' [8] According to Drayton, the church life cycle has three phases – growth, maintenance and terminal.

The growth phase usually lasts for approximately twenty-five years. During this phase the church grows by people transferring into it, as it is usually in a newer suburb. Transfer growth is replaced by biological growth as the children of earlier transferees grow, come to faith and join the church.

The growth phase is ultimately replaced by the maintenance phase which usually lasts for about twenty years. During this time the children, now grown up, marry and move out as it is usually too expensive for the younger ones to buy into their parents' suburbs. Those who remain opt for security and status quo. Evangelism slackens to occasional events which are more relevant to the congregation than to any outsider. Numbers plateau and gradually start to decline.

This usually results in the terminal phase in which an increasingly aging church membership locks itself comfortably into a predictable end – the death of the church. Although the church may still be surrounded by other people, the congregation, fully internalised and inward look-ing, no longer notices them or has a vision of reaching them.

Statistics and their analyses would clearly indicate that many churches are well advanced into the maintenance phase. Unless they want to preside over their own funerals, now is the time for turning around to seek God once more.

Death need not be inevitable. To break away from approaching the death cycle is a matter of choice and change. If the church will 'pray the price' it may live again. The option of death as compared to life is an important additional motivator for many.

Before leaving 'Motivation' to consider 'Inspiration' one important question must be answered – who will be the primary motivator? Who is the linchpin between motivation and inspiration? The answer is unavoidably – the pastor. Wagner says that 'if churches are going to maximise their growth potential they need pastors who are strong leaders.'[9]

They will certainly need to be leaders in personal and cor-porate prayer for the sake of their own personal spiritual health, as well as that of the churches they would seek to lead.

One of the more remarkable cases of all categories of church growth would be that of Spurgeon's Tabernacle dur-ing the life of its namesake. For example, according to that church's publication, *The Sword and Trowel*, by March 1891 the Tabernacle had grown in membership to 5,328 persons. Its lay members were serving around London in 127 centres. It operated an additional 23 mission stations with a total seating capacity for 4,000. It conducted 23 Sunday Schools with 600 teachers and 8,000 scholars. Also in that year it had opened another new church at Surrey Gardens to seat 1,000 people. All this flowed from (non-Pentecostal!) C.H. Spurgeon and the people he trained. The behind-the-scenes secret of Spurgeon's achievements is well summarised by Dinsdale, Young and Dallmore:

> 'Prayer was the instinct of his soul, and the atmosphere of his life. It was his "vital breath" and "native air".'[10]

'He knew that God's power was manifested in the services in proportion as God's people truly prayed and that in such proportion also souls were brought under conviction and drawn to Christ.'[11]

'The chief element of Spurgeon's entire career was his walk with God in prayer.'[12]

A key to growth becomes not just the pastor but the pastor's prayer life. As a river is unable to rise above its source, so a church will be unable to go spiritually 'above' its pastor. Similarly, pastors cannot lead where they have not first gone themselves.

For many centuries, the primary spiritual responsibilities of pastors have been recognised by the church. For example, in 817 the Council of Reform recommended that all clerics participate in seven or eight hours of prayer per day in addition to reciting all 150 Psalms thrice daily![13]

Many of today's pastors have quite a different orientation. In one American survey, when pastors were asked how long each prayed per day, 50 percent reported fifteen minutes, 20 percent said thirty minutes, and 5 percent said sixty minutes.[14] This sort of result would support the contention that

'many ... pastors ... live as though they consider prayer a last resort weapon in life's battles. If all else fails we get down on our knees ... We try things our way and when our way doesn't work, we cry out to God.'[15]

But pastors' prayer lives are vital to changing their own lives and those of their churches. Rarely, if ever, may a church be found to be praying (and growing) if its leadership is not praying.[16]

The problem for pastors today seems to be how they manage and prioritise the many demands made upon their time. Centuries ago, St Vincent De Paul succinctly warned that it was one of Satan's stratagems to so incite pastors 'to do more than they are able in order that they may no longer be able to do anything.'[17]

Where necessary, pastors should call for outside assistance to help them with time management. To ensure their priorities remain in order, especially that of prayer, they should hold themselves accountable to others.[18]

Pastors need to model prayer, not just for the sake of their churches, but even more so for their families (Proverbs 22:6). If the pastors' own children are lost what is left?

Apart from pastors' own prayer lives, they need to be willing to receive prayer from others. In recent years, C. Peter Wagner,[19] in lectures, seminars and articles, and at least one video tape (with John Maxwell of Skyline Wesleyan Church, Los Angeles), has done much to highlight the need for pastors and all church leaders to recruit teams of intercessors who will intercede for them personally. His most extensive treatment on the subject to date is his book, *Prayer Shield*.[20] Having recruited intercessors, it is vital for the pastor to provide for them aids such as monthly prayer bulletins, quarterly meetings and annual retreats, and to be available to them.

When the pastor is committed to prayer and the leaders become committed as well, then and only then can they expect the congregation to start to participate seriously in the church's prayer life.[21]

With pastors' prayer lives in order, we might then expect effective motivation which could lead to inspiration.

Inspiration

People are not inspired to pray by negative browbeating and by pastors denouncing their lack of prayer and evangelism.[22] They have enough self-induced guilt without pastors loading on more.

Many do not pray because of self-doubt. They can believe God responds to the prayers of others but not to theirs.[23] They do not want to remain the way they are. They will respond if motivated and inspired so to do. If people are motivated by a biblical understanding of who they are in Christ and what is the place of prayer, they are more easily able to be inspired. The simplest method is to tell stories of how prayer has worked for others.

It is easiest to start with the commonly accepted, authoritative, documented stories of others in the Bible. However, while it is good to reread the story of Moses and the Amalekites (Exodus 17:8–16), it is distant in time, and the magnitude of the supernatural involved renders difficult personal contemporary identification. It is probably better, therefore, to start with Peter's miraculous release from prison (Acts 12). Here was a group of everyday lay people praying about something close to their hearts, yet seemingly not expecting much to happen. When it did, they had difficulty believing and accepting it. Perhaps this was the founding congregation of the original 'Church of Saint Thomas'.

The average congregation of non-super-saints could certainly identify with those Jerusalem counterparts. It is important for the congregation to hear stories of common life, preferably from within their midst, of how God responds to the trials and tribulations of Mr or Mrs Average of suburbia or country farm.

Either the pastor does this as time permits over the pulpit, or an appointed prayer co-ordinator does it through church bulletin articles, newsletters, notice boards, or by the congregation themselves giving feedback through praise reports in service spots.

In October 1987, the Baptist Union of Australia in an attempt to kick-start evangelism through prayer triplets, published a pamphlet on the subject which went to all members of all churches within the Commonwealth. The pamphlet not only told of how prayer triplets could work, but provided anecdotal testimony. [24] The following year in their quarterly magazine, they were careful to continue the process, telling a continuous story of how converts were being won at the Aberfeldie Church in Melbourne. [25]

When, as mentioned earlier in this chapter, associate pastor Rod Denton returned from Korea and told an evening congregation of what God was doing through the prayer emphasis in that country, people, unannounced and uninvited, started spontaneously arriving at the church to pray at 4.00 a.m. the next morning. No call was made. They had simply been inspired by a credible witness telling of God doing great things through people just like themselves. Their doubt was overcome and they wanted changes in their lives, church, and nation, so they came to pray.

In addition to story sharing, annual seminars, books, films, and tracts should not be overlooked as appropriate sources for inspiration.

Ultimately to maintain effective prayer ministry, one is dependent upon the continual operation of the Holy Spirit. [26] However, a part of our responsibility is to maintain the flow of suitable information.

Information

Information may be conveyed through three media: visual, oral, and written. All three need to be used repeatedly.

Visual include video, slide, overhead projector, or film presentations. At every service reminders to pray should be given to the congregation by overhead transparency before, during and after services, and during 'free time'. Each month, video clips of three-minutes' duration can be shown during service slots. Longer videos of up to twenty-minutes' duration can be circulated among home groups. These are useful ways, especially for conveying points and background information on commissioning growth. A church's missionary staff should be expected to provide at least one three-minutes' video or slide presentation annually.

Written information requires special attention. In a generation which has been conditioned to receiving information visually in clips ranging from fifteen seconds to eight minutes through television outlets, written information, unless it is carefully, attractively presented and concisely stated, may be often consigned unread to the wastepaper basket along with the endless stream of unsolicited commercial 'junk mail'.

In the event of prayer letters, which all local and overseas missionary and pastoral staff should be urged to release on a frequency of once a month, these should not be more than one page in length. The page should consist of basically three paragraphs. Paragraph one may be personal news. Paragraph two should contain feedback on answers to previous prayer points. Paragraph three should contain the main prayer point for the month.

Repeated surveys over a number of years have shown that (busy) people who are already on information overload, often do not use or even read that which is longer than one page in presentation.

Prayer request and answer slips may also be used briefly in congregational prayer times, but more extensively in designated prayer rooms where the information can be available at all times to those who are praying. Collection points for such prayer slips may be the offering containers or specially designated boxes in the foyer.

It is important that the prayer slips be available in the foyer of the church for easy accessibility and high profile. They are so designed to allow for one item of information which is to be expressed in about twenty words, with all requestors being required to identify themselves by signing the slip. This eliminates wastage through bogus requests and keeps responsibility for disclosure of information on the person making the request.

Oral prayer information may be conveyed briefly during congregational service times, at prayer retreats, or through telephone prayer chains. If a church is divided into geographical regions prayer chains may be developed in every region, each with its own area co-ordinator. They can be activated usually to deal with crisis issues of physical health, relational breakdowns, financial traumas, and the like. Because of the well-known tendency for misinformation to develop with transmission of the message from one person to another, guidelines for each participant will be necessary. These may be:

1. The prayer chain is activated through the regional co-ordinator who asks, 'Exactly what do you want us to pray?' This request should be recorded in writing.
2. Each participant should write down the request.
3. Each person should pray over the matter as soon as possible after receiving the information.
4. Each should immediately phone the next person on the prayer chain and pass on the written information without elaboration.
5. If the person next on the prayer chain is uncontactable, the telephoner should pass on down the list until contact is made with the next available person.
6. The last person on the list should recontact the prayer co-ordinator. (This indicates how quickly and accurately the information was transmitted.)
7. No contact should be made with the person for whom prayer has been requested.
8. Prayer requests remain confidential.
9. If further information is needed or desired, contact can be made with the regional prayer co-ordinator or pastor.

With written prayer information processes especially, it is important that procedures and participants be reviewed regularly for two reasons. Firstly, people tend to make a higher commitment if they know when the endpoint is. Secondly, recipients of prayer information are usually too embarrassed to notify the senders when they do not wish to continue their commitment. This would appear to be 'unspiritual'. Thus much written material is wasted because of lack of review procedures which give participants opportunities to continue or discontinue.

In processing all information, its content and frequency of release needs constant, careful monitoring to evaluate whether or not it is effective communication.

Communication

Vision and a pastor's ability to communicate that vision have frequently been cited (along with prayer) as among the most important factors in church growth. [27]

Components of vision are faith and tenacity. To see it come to pass not only must pastors pray it in, they must persevere with their congregations, constantly communicating vision within a prayer context. Media specialists advise that it takes on average almost six exposures to information until communication is effected.

At Blackburn Baptist in Melbourne, Australia, in the lead up to a Christmas appeal for Third World needs in 1990, even after three church bulletin presentations, not even the office staff who typed, printed, and distributed those bulletins could recall the stated reason for the appeal. The parable of the persistent widow which Jesus told (Luke 18:1–8), is not only applicable to perseverance to obtain justice, it may also apply at a human level to indicate what is required to get and maintain the attention of the desired audience.

Jonathan Edwards promoted prayer to his generation. He also challenged them to maintain monthly special prayer meetings for seven years, then to evaluate and to keep on. Judging by the response, one must conclude that Edwards was an effective pray-er, promoter, mobiliser, inspirer, and communicator of the vision and the needs God had placed upon his heart. If we would see happen in our day what happened in Edwards's day, we should aspire to be and to do likewise.

Location

At some point, the loftiest of spiritual visions will need to commence to take shape through a succession of mundane practical steps in the realm of the physical. Prayer ministry is no exception. Amongst the earliest questions to be answered are, With whom and where will one pray? This needs to be addressed at the personal, local, and regional levels.

In former times pastors and people had their 'prayer closets' at home and in the church sanctuary. However, in modern western homes with a premium on space, privacy, and family entertainment, such 'closets' are no longer a part of standard architectural design.

Similarly in the church, where cost effectiveness and high usage factors prevail, the traditional 'sanctuary' has become a multipurpose auditorium. In either place, to reserve space exclusively dedicated for prayer is going to be a costly exercise. However, as annual budgets should reflect a church's priorities, so should its architecture, construction, and space allocations. It comes down in practice to what priority we are really ready to give prayer in our personal and corporate lives.

None of this is to gainsay the primacy of the condition of one's heart over all else in coming to pray, but these practical considerations must be addressed and resolved as early as possible in the process.

At the personal level, one may opt for such places as the family car, a garden seat in the park, the lounge room at 2.00 a.m., or whatever is personally convenient. Obviously as there is only one person involved (and any movement is only as strong as the individuals who comprise it), whatever is convenient and available is suitable. What is important is to settle upon a time and a place where one will daily 'meet with the Lord'.

At the local level, again contemporary pastors face challenges which were not part of their predecessors' world. If they are fortunate enough not to have to meet in multi-shared, hired public facilities, but actually to have facilities owned by the churches, it is unlikely there will be easily available space to locate a prayer centre.

The ideal is to have available a room of suitable size which is easily accessible 168 hours per week without mutual disruption of intercessors and whoever else is using church facilities. Sometimes this will require sensitive, patient interdepartmental negotiation to achieve this ideal space. Blessed is the church which includes space for a 'prayer chapel' which is exclusively used for that purpose, and so designed and located to allow for easy access and exit without interfacing with any other on-site activity.

This approach assumes, of course, that the site of the congregation's worship centre is the most appropriate and convenient place. In larger urban 'regional' churches this may not be the case. In the post Second World War period, with the spread of private vehicle ownership and freeway systems, many pastors no longer have easily defined geographical areas. Baby boomer or baby buster consumerism is coming to affect the choice of church almost as much as it does the choice of goods on supermarket shelves. Therefore, the pastor ought not to conclude automatically that where the church is located is the obvious place for a prayer ministry site.

If the objective is to maximise prayer participation rather than collecting people together in one location, multi-sites are preferable. Relational networking clusters usually have greater attraction than centrally organised functions. Whether the relationship is friendship or common task based, participation rates for relationally oriented events usually surpass those of other sorts.

Pastors may need to overcome their natural inclinations to organise and control centrally, rather than take the healthy risk of faith to allow people to gather to pray by themselves. John Dawson puts the principle succinctly when he says:

> 'God's kingdom is a kingdom of liberty in which everything is permitted unless specifically prohibited. Satan's kingdom is a controlled hierarchy in which nothing is permitted unless authorised. God ... can safely decentralise without losing control; Satan fears the loss of control and draws everything into a pyramid of power with himself at the centre.' [28]

The other aspect of location which pastors especially need to consider is that which applies beyond their immediate vicinity. Without debating the related issues of structure and uniformity, in general terms, it is true to say that God desires unity amongst his people (John 17:11; Ephesians 4:3). History is replete with sufficient examples of enhanced spiritual power whenever individual and groups of churches have acted in unison. In each great move of the Spirit referred to earllier in chapter three, praying in unity was one of the common characteristics which preceded and maintained such movements. The same is true today. [29]

Again, John Dawson [30] relates how during the Los Angeles Olympics he and others participated in a prayer and outreach thrust involving 1,600 churches and prayer networks around the world. Pastors, para-church groups, congregations, and 300,000 intercessors in Korea, gathered frequently for city-wide concerts of united prayer, focused on Los Angeles. Dawson reported the following benefits:

1. Christian leaders were able to discern and break more easily Satan's power over the city.
2. People in general seemed more cheerful and friendly across the city.
3. Summer traffic jams and pollution failed to materialise.
4. Incidence of serious crime fell dramatically. The city morgue, which normally received on average seventy-eight bodies per day, many the result of murders, reported that during the period of the Olympics there were no murder victims.
5. An estimated one thousand people per day were accepting Jesus Christ as Lord.

Pastors need to lead their people beyond their local boundaries, seeking to harmonise and unite with others who have larger visions of what united prayer can do in the body of Christ. Lessons from Christian history indicate that this is a preliminary condition for church growth of exponential proportions.

Implementation

The end of talking is the beginning of action. The end of theory is the beginning of practice. In practice one should expect mistakes to be made. This is one of the surest ways of learning and, therefore, should be accepted as a positive experience on the path of improvement. The important thing is to avoid making the same mistakes twice. Ultimately, each church or group of people will need to determine by trial and error what works best for them. For example, the Solomon Island practice of 4.00 a.m. prayer meetings mentioned earlier with respect to the Palm Beach Baptist Church, was found quickly to be non-transferable from the South Pacific islands to urban Australia.

In the islands, the more subsistence economy based on fishing and food gathering according to need allowed for a more relaxed lifestyle. Solomon Islanders, following their usual practice, went back to bed to sleep for a few hours later in the morning, while their more regimented Australian counterparts had to go off to start work for the day! Heroic praying in the pre-dawn hours had to give way to more pragmatic necessities. Candles burning at both ends have a very diminished useful life expectancy.

What may 'work'?

Some things which commonly 'work' and which may prove useful elsewhere include:

1. Monday to Friday 6.00 a.m. prayer meetings focusing on for example, local, state and federal government authorities, local outreach, countries in which a church has missionaries and so on.
2. Saturday 6.00 a.m. men's prayer meetings (men return to their families before the children are awake).
3. Ladies' early afternoon meetings (younger children are at school during this time).
4. Sunday 4.00 p.m. weekly youth department meetings (this is the time when most young people are available before coming to the evening service).
5. Prayer prior to and during Sunday services.

6. Monday 8.00 a.m. staff prayer meetings.
7. Tuesday to Friday 9.00 a.m. staff prayer meetings.
8. Prayer requests retrieved from foyer receptacles can be prayed over at the Sunday evening services then forwarded to the prayer room for daily prayer.
9. For missionary staff:
    (a) Once a month evening prayer meetings.
    (b) Overhead transparency reminders at each church service.
    (c) Mention in pulpit pastoral prayers each Sunday morning service.
    (d) Distribution of prayer letters to members of the congregation can be encouraged.
    (e) Each missionary member may be adopted by one or more home groups for prayer and other support.
    (f) Global wall-mounted prayer maps can be displayed in the auditorium foyer and the pastor's office.
    (g) Audio or video cassettes can be played monthly at Sunday services and then released to circulate through home groups.
    (h) A day of prayer and fasting can be held at the time of the annual missionary convention.
10. Monthly prayer services exclusively for physical healing.
11. Monthly half-nights of prayer (8.00–12.00) for the state of the church.
12. Weekly prayer meetings for pastors on Monday afternoons; (they probably don't feel like doing much else on Mondays!).
13. Twice yearly retreats for pastors, each for two to three days.
14. Annual two-day prayer retreats for lay leadership members.
15. Annual two-day separate retreats for various departments.
16. Prayer chains in each geographical region activated for any crisis matter.

17. Intercessor groups for each pastor (groups should receive monthly prayer letters and meet with their pastor quarterly and on other occasions).
18. Each pastor might take time out for a monthly day of prayer and fasting.
19. Prayer triplets for evangelism.
20. Identifying exceptionally gifted intercessors to link them together into their own groups to function on a meta-church model on behalf of the whole church.

To maintain a priority on prayer:

1. Organise annual seminars on prayer.
2. Provide monthly prayer bulletins covering all major issues and departments in the church.
3. Use in services overhead transparency prayer reminders (weekly), video or audio spots (monthly), and give mini-teaching series on prayer (annually).
4. Ensure that the church bookshop is well stocked with a variety of books on and aids to prayer.

To maintain a modicum of direction and momentum, prayer co-ordinators need to be appointed. The co-ordinators need to know precisely what their roles are and where they fit into the scheme of things. Each needs a job description and organisational flow chart for guidance. [31]

Special care needs to be given to maintain the attractiveness of larger all-day or all-night prayer meetings. All-night prayer meetings are best scheduled on Friday nights to allow for recuperation on Saturday. Because of late night shopping in most urban centres, it is inadvisable to commence before 9.00 p.m. on a 'come when you can, leave when you must' basis.

The following timetable may prove helpful:

Sample Prayer Meeting Timetable

Time	*Activity*
9.00–9.30 p.m.	Praise and worship
9.30–10.00	Teaching on prayer
10.00–10.30	Listening and recording what the Spirit might be saying

10.30–11.00	Sharing and discerning
11.00–12.00	Praying over whatever is discerned
12.00–12.30 a.m.	Coffee and biscuits
12.30–1.00	Praise and worship
1.00–2.00	Praying for the church
2.00–3.00	Praying for the community, state and nation
3.00–4.00	Praying for church staff and missionaries
4.00–4.30	Coffee and biscuits
4.30–5.00	Listening to the Holy Spirit
5.00–5.45	The world and any special items
5.45–6.00 a.m.	Praise, thanksgiving and worship

For prayer meetings of longer duration it is advisable to:
1. Change leaders at regular intervals
2. Break up into changing clusters of small groups, and
3. Allow for appropriately spaced rest breaks.

To maintain interest and enthusiasm, arrange for key prayer leaders to visit other churches which are growing and have effective prayer ministries.

Evaluation

The final step in developing a church-wide prayer ministry is evaluation.

How many people are participating?

What results are being achieved with regard to such goals as healing, evangelism, or missionary appointees?

Just as the 'unexamined life is not worth living', so an unevaluated programme is not worth pursuing.

In prayer ministry we pursue not mere maintenance of the status quo, but real quantitative and qualitative growth within the church.

Hesselgrave believes that in outreach, prayer is more than a starting point: 'It is the continuing force behind the entire programme of outreach.'[32]

There is another simple reason outreach occurs whenever

people start to pray for the conversion of others. Brian Mills found that when people start to pray for others they tend 'to become the answer to their own praying.'[33] That experience is not unique to prayer triplets in England.

In 1968, Evelyn Christenson was the national women's chairperson for the Baptist General Conference's involvement in the Crusade of the Americas. She was also appointed to lead prayer for evangelism in her own church in Rockford, Illinois. She determined to lead in prayer for twelve months, after which evangelism would be carried out for the next twelve months.

However, within six months she was reporting that a transition had taken place in her church. They found that people who prayed automatically evangelised. Their whole church became increasingly evangelistic, not because of the external superimposition of programmes but because of a change of heart from within praying workers.

Her husband's conclusion was, 'A praying church is an evangelising church.'[34]

Endnotes

1. Rod Denton, 'Asian Trip August 18 – September 7. 1985.' TMs. September 1985, Blackburn Baptist Church Archives, Melbourne. 5.

2. Terry Tekyl, *Pray and Grow*. Nashville, Tennessee: Discipleship Resources, 1988, 4.

3. J. Hesselgrave, *Planting Churches Cross-Culturally*. Grand Rapids, Michigan: Baker, 1978. 146.

4. Mark Buckley, 'Lessons From Desert Storm,' *Ministries Today*, May/June 1991, 110.

5. David Bryant, *Prayer Pacesetters Sourcebook*. Minneapolis, Minnesota: Concerts of Prayer International, 1989, 94.

6. Wesley L. Duewel, *Touch the World through Prayer*. Grand Rapids, Michigan: Francis Asbury Press, 1978, 25.

7. B.J. Willhite, 'How to Get Your People to Pray,' *Ministries Today*, November/December 1988, 32–37.

8. Dean Drayton, 'Life or Death.' *On Being*, June 1986, 7.

9. C. Peter Wagner, *Leading Your Church To Growth*. Ventura, California: Regal Books, 1984, 73.

10. T. Dinsdale and C.H. Young, *Spurgeon's Prayers*. New York: Revell, 1906, vi.

11. A. Dallmore, *C.H. Srurgeon*. Chicago: Moody Press, 1984, 48.

12. *Ibid.*, 177.

13. Terry Muck. *Liberating the Leader's Prayer Life*. Waco, Texas: Word Books, 1985, 18.

14. Terry Muck, 'Ten Questions About the Devotional Life,' *Leadership*. Winter 1982, 34.

15. Robert E. Logan, *Beyond Church Growth*. Old Tappan, New Jersey: Fleming H. Revell, 1989, 32.

16. Dick Eastman, *Change the World School of Prayer*. Penshurst, NSW: World Literature Crusade, 1983, 19.

17. Terry Muck, *Liberating the Leader's Prayer Life*, 192.

18. *Ibid.*, 163.

19. C. Peter Wagner, 'Praying for Leaders.' *Equipping the Saints*, Spring 1990. 23–27.

20. C. Peter Wagner, *Prayer Shield*. Ventura, California: Regal Books, 1992.

21. Paul Cedar, 'A Pastor's Perspective of Building a Praying Church.' In *Unleashing the Power of Prayer*, ed. Vonette Bright and Ben A. Jennings, Chicago: Moody Press, 1989, 195.

22. Reg Klimionok, *Levels of Church Growth*. Slacks Creek, Queensland: Assembly Press, 1984, 182.

23. B.J. Willhite, *Why Pray?* Altamonte Springs, Florida: Creation House, 1988, 18.

24. 'Cross Over Australia, Baptists Together in Evangelism.' Spring 1987, 4–5.

25. 'Worthwhile and Exciting,' *National Baptist*, September 1988, 14; 'Prayer Triplets Bring Joy,' *National Baptist*, December 1988, 15.

26. John Dawson, *Taking Our Cities For God*. Kilsyth, Victoria, Australia: Word, 1989, 207.

27. Logan, *Beyond Church Growth*, 34.

28. Dawson, *Taking Our Cities For God*, 103.

29. Francis Frangipane. *The House of the Lord*. Milton Keynes, England: Word Publishing, 1992, 145–153.

30. Dawson, *Taking Our Cities for God*, 71–73.

31. See Appendices 2 and 3 respectively.

32. Hesselgrave, *Planting Churches Cross-Culturally*, 146.

33. Brian Mills, *Three Times Three Equals Twelve*. Eastbourne, Sussex: Kingsway, 1986, 29.
34. Evelyn Christenson, *What Happens When Women Pray*. Wheaton, Illinois: Victor Books, 1975, 118.

Chapter 7

Push On

Bob Logan ought to know what he is talking about. Although he currently works as a consultant with Church Resource Ministries, prior to that he was the founding pastor of Community Baptist Church in Alta Loma, California. During his eleven years with the church, it grew to a worship attendance of more than 1,200 people. Community Baptist also planted six other churches in 1984–88, some of which have since planted others. [1]

After considerable study and practical experience, Logan is of the opinion that 'even in the best of churches, health that produces growth is not natural in the sense that it is spontaneous or automatic. It carefully must be planned for, nurtured, worked hard for, monitored and exploited.' [2] This observation applies not only to overall growth in the church but to each of its departments. The whole can never be greater than the sum of its parts any more than a chain can be stronger than its weakest link.

It is desirable, therefore, not only to have the whole church covered, protected, and nurtured by prayer, but the same also needs to apply to each of its departments. Equally, each department needs to be developed by Spirit-guided planning processes. The development of prayer ministry is no exception.

Spiritual planning will produce spiritual results even for such a 'spiritual' work as prayer. To develop prayer ministry to facilitate church growth, a way through the maze of options of sanctified, applied commonsense may unfold as follows:

1.   Purpose
2.   Goal setting
3.   Prioritising
4.   Planning
5.   Obstacles and opportunities
6.   Specific Goals.

Purpose

If we neither know nor care where we are going, any road may get us there. Alternatively, we may settle down to the giddying prospect of endless circles. We need to provoke ourselves by asking critical questions: for example, Why are we living? What is God's will for the church? What is the purpose of prayer ministry?

Purpose is the 'why' of what we are doing. It is not necessarily measurable in itself but it does set a clear, long-term direction for our lives. 'Purpose or mission governs our lives.' [3]

Our purpose in living and working is the foundation on which our goals are built. Without goals we are unlikely to develop, administer or lead an effective prayer ministry department.

Goal Setting

If we aim at nothing, that is probably what we will hit. The urgent will displace the important. We will major on minors. Instead of aiming to achieve goals we have set, the demands of others will mostly determine the course of our lives.

A goal is a statement of faith about the future in accordance with a vision or calling God has given for the development and establishment of any ministry. It will be within the context of purpose. It identifies more specifically what God has shown and for what we are believing him. Goals are means to ends, not ends in themselves. They are meant to be our servants, not our masters. They are certainly not unspiritual when they help us to move according to God's revealed purposes for our ministries.

Jesus himself seemed to move with deliberate purpose and goals in mind. He said,

> *'Let us go to the next town that I may preach there also, for this is why I came.'*   (Mark 1:37–38)

When he was praying to the Father, he said,

> *'I have accomplished the work you gave me to do.'*
>   (John 17:4)

Obviously he knew what was intended for him to achieve day by day and year by year.

It was similar for the Apostle Paul. He said,

> *'I press on toward the goal to win the prize for which God has called me heavenward in Christ Jesus.'*
>   (Philippians 3:14)

To his disciple Timothy he wrote,

> *'I have fought the good fight, I have finished the race, I have kept the faith.'*   (2 Timothy 4:7)

Paul was a person who knew what God expected of him and set about doing it with minimal deflection.

Whether it was Noah building an ark, Moses leading his people toward the promised land, Joshua or David overcoming enemy forces in Israel, Solomon building the Temple, or Nehemiah rebuilding Jerusalem, each knew what their goals were.

Rather than do many things poorly, they concentrated on doing a few things well. Hence the specification in the preceding chapter regarding an appointee to be prayer co-ordinator states that the person would need to relinquish all other responsibilities in the church to concentrate on doing this one thing well.

If a church or ministry is to grow, every opportunity needs to be taken to set goals according to God's purposes rather than being dominated by our own daily, lesser concerns.

Dayton and Engstrom[4] list ten good reasons for setting goals in the church. They say that goals:

1. Give a sense of direction and purpose.
2. Give us the power to live in the present.
3. Promote enthusiasm and strong organisational life.
4. Help us to evaluate our progress.
6. Force us to plan ahead.
7. Help us to communicate within the organisation.
8. Give people a clear understanding of what is expected.
9. Help us to reduce needless conflict and duplication of effort.
10. Take the emphasis off activity and place it on output.

Goal setting forces us down to the reality that we have to do something new and make decisions toward implementing what we have undertaken to do on behalf of the church; namely, to build a prayer ministry which will undergird the whole of the church's growth.

If goal setting is so significant, why then do we avoid it? For most other areas of our lives we often have unspoken short- and long-term goals. For example, every day we try to reach places of employment, to earn money, to pay bills, to feed, clothe and educate children who are nurtured toward ultimate independence.

If goal setting is so significant, why avoid it in the church or church department? The commonest reason may be fear of failure and the damage to our pride, embarrassment, or rejection by others which may result. Jesus spoke strongly against such an attitude (Matthew 25:25). Without the possibility of failure and some risk, no faith is exercised, which is hardly pleasing to God (Hebrews 11:6).

A second common reason for avoiding goal setting may be an innate sense of inadequacy or incompetence. However, if our goal is to please God (2 Corinthians 5:9), our confidence is not in ourselves (Philippians 3:3). Our confidence and competence is in God (2 Corinthians 3:4–8).

In formulating goals for the prayer ministry, it needs to be ensured that they are:

1. Biblical: this brings them into line with 'purpose'.
2. Measurable: so that it can be known whether or not they are being attained.
3. Attainable: they are to be big enough to inspire and challenge, but small enough to reach.
4. Relevant: to fit within the vision and the philosophy of ministry of the whole church.
5. Owned: good goals are my goals, bad goals tend to be someone else's goals. We usually act only on what we own.
6. Communicated: so that others will come to own them as well.
7. Written down: so they will not be forgotten.
8. Prioritised: we cannot do everything at once.

In the whole area of goal setting it is important to remember that there needs to be a faith component to stretch a church beyond that which is within its own span of control. Every church needs to be challenged beyond mere maintenance. We need to aim for growth and be moving toward impossibility fringes which oblige us to rely upon the providence of God.

Senior pastor John Wimber of Vineyard Ministries, often says in his seminars that faith is spelt 'r-i-s-k'. That has potential to hurt. However, as his neighbouring church growth seminar leader Robert Schuller often adds, 'There can be no gain without pain.' The sort of goals which are needed are those which honour God, meet real human need, grip the imagination of the congregation, and challenge faith, providing they are not beyond the church's or the department's current faith capacity level.

Jesus said,

> *'According to your faith will it be done to you.'*
>
> (Matthew 9:29)

Prioritising

In the prayer ministry department, as in any human organisation, not everything can be done simultaneously. Everything may be good, but not everything will be 'best'. From a range of options, a choice has to be made of what to do first and in what order will tasks be done or allocated. By the choices we make, we prioritise.

When Jesus said that he accomplished the work that his Father had given him to do (John 17:4), he would have known that there was still much which had not been done in terms of introducing or completing the work of the kingdom of God. It was obvious that he had not just been responding to the exigencies of the moment or the endless needs of others, but that he had been working according to priorities set before him by his Father. That was especially so in the practice of prayer (Mark 1:35; Luke 6:12; Matthew 26:46–44).

Blaise Pascal once said that the last thing that most of us learn is what should be first. Progress toward goals is achieved by prioritising tasks and concentrating on the completion of each before progressing to the next. [5]

Setting of priorities takes on extra importance especially in the initial stages of establishing a new ministry. If the person selected to become prayer co-ordinator is inexperienced in administrative technique, it will be very important for the pastor to give time to help set priorities and thus reduce the anxiety state of the new worker. For the first month or two the pastor might even need to set a 'to do' list [6] to help forge a way forward until the new co-ordinator gets a feel for the scope of and the time needed for the ministry.

A well-known series of events in church history exemplifies the importance of prioritising for church growth.

In the thirteenth century there existed one of the greatest empires which the world had ever seen up to that time. It was that of Mogul emperor Kublai Khan. The empire stretched from the Ural mountains in the north, to the Himalayas in the south; from the China Sea in the east, to Europe in the west.

In the year 1271 Kublai Khan sent back to Europe Nicolo and Maffeo Polo whom he had appointed as his ambassadors to the Pope in Rome. The Great Khan requested that the Pope send one hundred men who could teach the truths of Christianity so that the Emperor and all of his nobles could understand this 'new' religion. Kublai Khan correctly surmised that when this was done, should he and his courtiers accept the faith, Christians in his empire would outnumber the total of all others elsewhere.

Unfortunately, the Roman hierarchy was so preoccupied at that time with internal maintenance matters that they missed completely this unprecedented and irrepeatable church growth opportunity. For eighteen years no response was forthcoming from the Roman church leadership. Then in 1289 a handful of missionaries were sent – too few, too late and the chance was gone. This happened either because the church leadership failed to prioritise its tasks, or it had no plan for outreach and growth.

> *'For want of a skilful strategy an army is lost; victory is the fruit of long planning.'* (Proverbs 11:14 NEB)

Planning

Well-known international American entertainer Diana Ross is reported to have said, 'I feel like I'm walking around in this circle and I'm pacing and I don't feel like I can get anything done.'[7] Many Christians in leadership have felt the same way because they have failed to spend time in prioritised planning. They don't plan to fail. They just fail to plan and often the end result is the same – failure.

While priorities give us an order of action and goals give us direction in terms of purpose, to implement them planning is needed. Planning is trying to discover how to accomplish goals before one is committed to a course of action. It is moving from the 'now' to the 'then', from the way things are to the way we want them to be. It is trying to imagine the future as we would like it to be and explaining how to get there. 'Plan in advance how a job is done and it is already half done' says Dayton. [8] For the Christian, this becomes a matter of trying to understand God's will and then responding to it by actions we take. If a church's prayer ministry is to affect the future, it ought to do so with godly purpose rather than by random reactionary thrusts. [9]

If the planning process is so important, why is it not usually applied to the development of prayer ministries?

Probably because of:

1. The tyranny of the urgent.

   We so easily become preoccupied with responding to demands of the present, that we neglect to give adequate attention to what we want to achieve in the future. Planning helps to divert from the immediately urgent to the ultimately important, so that we no longer manage by crisis.

2. The power of precedents: 'We've never done it that way before.'

3. The fear of failure.

   This may be neutralised by asking, 'What if we succeed?'

4. Excessive busyness.

   We need to challenge one another and question the effectiveness of such busyness in terms of goals and priorities.

5. It is 'unspiritual' or 'unbiblical'. It will erode our complete dependence upon God.

   To the unthinking, this line of argument would apply especially to the establishment of prayer ministries which in appearance must be about the most 'spiritual' activity that one could imagine. Zechariah 4:6–7 and James 4:13–16 are often quoted in support of this criticism. However, these and other similar passages emphasise wrong attitudes rather than preclude the possibility of planning. They rightly warn against relying solely upon our own ingenuity.

In working to develop a prayer ministry both to clear the way for and undergird church growth, we need to use all the gifts with which God has endowed his people. Certainly that which is unique to humans is our ability to think, plan, and work toward long-term future goals. We do this for all other areas of our lives so why not in the church and its prayer ministries?

The only event which may happen without any human assistance or intervention is death, and even that is being challenged with the increased popularity of euthanasia in certain western countries. To maintain life and growth requires constant attention and effort on our part. Besides, all plans that we make are only provisional and remain dependent upon the grace and energy of God for their fulfilment. That principle certainly must apply to the growth of the church which is of supernatural origin and sustenance.

There is no way that Jacob, Joseph, or David could have risen to greatness and achieved what God wanted to do through them, without due consideration as to what their future courses of action needed to be. The same could be said of Paul with his church-planting missionary strategies.

God himself seems to work carefully step by step (Isaiah 48:3–5). Certain things he has determined from the beginning (Ephesians 1:5), and toward that end, in an orderly fashion, he continues to *'work out everything in conformity with the purpose of his will'*, (Ephesians 1:11). He has plans for the whole world (Matthew 25:34; Galatians 4:4; Ephesians 4:1–10). He regards us as his fellow workers (2 Corinthians 6:1). He delegates to us as co-labourers responsible for the execution of his plans, and expects us to exercise our judgment and to accept responsibilities (Psalm 32:8–9).

In the story about houses built upon sand and rock, in part, Jesus may be saying that we need to give careful thought in advance to the outcome of our actions (Luke

6:46–49). Elsewhere, Jesus criticised those who foolishly failed to think ahead clearly (Luke 14:28–30). Not only may we be required to plan, but we will also be held accountable for our actions (Matthew 25:14–30). So it is not just a matter of, say, making an announcement in church that a prayer meeting is going to be started and then sitting back to see what happens.

Purpose tells us why we want to do something. Goals explain where and within what time we want to achieve something. Planning is the step needed to attain the goals and answers the question, 'How do we want to get there?'

The planning process in its simplest form results from asking questions and setting out answers on a sheet of paper. The questions may be:

1. What goal do we want to reach?
2. What is the last thing which has to happen before that goal is accomplished? (It is necessary to work backwards from where we want to be to where we are.)
3. Within what time does each task need to be completed?
4. Who will be responsible for each task?
5. To achieve this what resources are needed in terms of equipment, accommodation, money, or personnel?
6. What are the obstacles or opportunities which will hinder each phase?

In planning, the following guidelines have proved helpful:

1. Schedule regular times for planning and review.

   Time spent at the beginning of ministry development saves time later, enhances results, and gives increased job satisfaction.

2. Do it prayerfully

   We need to know what God wants and how he wants it done, more than we need to know what others want of us.

3. Remain flexible.

   Plans are servants, not masters. They need to be reviewed regularly and, where necessary, adjusted to new information or circumstances. It is usually imposs-ible to know everything from the beginning.

4.   Make sure plans reflect purpose, goals, and priorities.
5.   Allow for interruptions.

> *'In his heart a man plans his course, but the Lord determines his steps.'*   (Proverbs 6:9)

6.   Communicate plans and negotiate their acceptance by those to whom one is accountable, as well as with those who are accountable to the planner.
7.   Discipline will be required.
     Plan the work and work the plan. It is better to win control over oneself than over whole cities (Proverbs 16:32).
8.   Leave the results to God.
     If we commit our ways to him our plans will succeed (Proverbs 16:3), often in spite of obstacles or even missed opportunities.

Obstacles and Opportunities

Reporting on the amazing changes which are occurring for the church in Eastern Europe in general and Romania in particular, Ginger Hope wrote that impact is being made by people and churches who 'still dare to make plans and dream'.[10] These churches have had to overcome many obstacles and learn to recognise and seize the slightest opportunity just to maintain their existence for much of the preceding four to seven decades.

To develop an effective prayer base for church growth, there will be a similar need to overcome obstacles and capitalise on opportunities, or better still, to turn obstacles into opportunities.

Three common obstacles are:

1. General ignorance about the strategic importance of prayer and the urgent need for specific prayer to facilitate growth

As outlined in Chapter 6 under 'Motivation', this is an

opportunity to teach people about God, his ways, expectations, and where we fit in. Terry Teykl sees teaching about prayer evangelism as priority number one. He goes even further by asserting that no prayer events should even be scheduled until education of the people through a teaching programme has been accomplished.[11]

2. The general spiritual condition of the one who prays

For example, a person's ability and willingness to pray may be affected by unconfessed sin, rebelliousness, overcommitment in other areas of life and work, or even just plain laziness.

Karl Barth said, 'We are not free to pray or not to pray, nor to pray only when we feel so inclined.'[12] That being so, even personal and private issues such as these need to be addressed and rectified.

There is no doubt that prayer can be hard work (Colossians 4:12–13). If we want to hear God with a view to working with him to formulate and implement his plans for church growth, then prayer becomes mandatory. There is no other option. Its practice can never therefore, be left to the mercy of feelings or emotional states. It is a matter of decision, of the will, to determine to obey or not, and then remaining sufficiently disciplined to commence and continue up to when the grace of God draws us with such power that we would have it no other way.

3. Discouragement

This comes about for practical reasons such as either too few turn up to pray, or if they do come in adequate numbers they quickly lose interest and fall away again when prayed-for results are not quickly forthcoming. It may also come about because of things happening within the one who comes to pray, such as self-condemnation whenever one falls into sin.

The first may be muted by ensuring that there is adequate feedback of positive results. If there are none initially in the local church, then stories from elsewhere should be shared.

Even better is to send those who pray to where positive things are already happening, to receive encouragement to continue.

It is important that the guardian of the church's prayer ministry vision, the (senior) pastor, be constantly affirming and encouraging his people by example, presence, notes, or in any way possible. In between times, when we are waiting upon God to move, it is important for people to be reminded that in God's kingdom nothing they do is ever in vain (1 Corinthians 15:58). Their prayers have ascended to the very presence of God (Revelation 5:8). He will certainly answer, although for some reason there may be delays (Daniel 9:23; 10:12–14). There is a need to persevere (Hebrews 10:35–38), because with the Lord *'a thousand years are like a day'* (2 Peter 3:8).

Regarding the more personal causes of spiritual discouragement, while these may not be able to be condoned, people should not be overly condemned. People need to be reminded that forgiveness is available (1 John 1:9); that our God is a God of the second chance (Jonah 3:1); that having received God's forgiveness, they need to forgive and accept themselves and move forward once more.

King David's life is a great encouragement in this regard. He was a person who prayed but whose spiritual journey through life was anything but constantly upward. He committed adultery, organised manslaughter, presided over disastrous developments in his family, some of which were attributable to him, and sometimes took major decisions without consulting with God. However, his redeeming feature was he knew how to repent and start out all over again.

> 'For any of us spiritual growth is not a steadily increasing incline but more a bumpy climb. Overall improvement is visible when seen from a distance – but it's hard won and uneven ... too often setbacks dominate us.' [13]

As with any worthwhile enterprise, undoubtedly there will be other obstacles. Many will be internal to the church, of its own making, because no church easily frees itself from its past weaknesses to change overnight. The important thing is that with faith and perseverance, most obstacles can be recycled into opportunities to keep us heading toward our goals in God.

Specific Goals

The specifics of a complete plan with goals which may be developed for prayer ministry for a particular church are not that useful for elsewhere. In fact they could be counterproductive. The danger frequently is that when one group of people see comparative success elsewhere, they try to revive their flagging fortunes by transferring what they have seen elsewhere into their own situation without amendment. It is always hoped that the ailing body will be revived instantly with this undiluted transfusion of new life. The problem is that it seldom works, because what is more important than the practice are the principles which guide practice.

This chapter has been about the practice of principles. Nevertheless, in spite of known hazards, one or two numbers may be tentatively mentioned as specific goals for membership involvement in any church's prayer ministry. Peter Wagner rightly urges that such be set by the senior pastor. [14]

Abundant Life Community Church in Pasadena, California, reached a figure of 21 percent of its Sunday congregation in cumulative attendance at its various prayer meetings throughout the week. Yoido Full Gospel Church in Seoul, Korea, involves 22 percent. Church on the Rock in Rockwall, Texas, reached 24 percent congregational participation in attendance at prayer meetings. (These figures were true for 1989.) [15]

Two important things to note from these figures are, that the amount of congregational involvement in each is above 20 percent, and that all three have been strongly growing churches. Therefore, it seems that a preliminary numerical goal which pastors could adopt, no matter how long-term it seems, is to have at least 20 percent of the congregation involved in some form or other, praying corporately for conversion growth through the church.

A Warning

Much of this chapter, of necessity, has been involved with technical and practical principles applicable for the development of prayer ministry to pave the way for church growth. However, it needs to be said that plans and suchlike are meant to inspire rather than dominate or manipulate people. People are more important than plans. People are the church. Plans are only meant to be scaffolding, as an aid to new 'building'. Therefore, plans are always meant to be subservient to the needs of people. Good plans, like goals, obstacles, and opportunities, are meant to keep us on our toes or, where necessary, to drive us to our knees.

If any church is to grow, it will usually need to break away from some of its traditional thinking and practice of its past. In confronting church growth, some may see it as sociological calculations, organisational management, marketing, advertising, public relations, propaganda, working the angles, figuring the odds, or minimising the risks so as to ensure institutional success. However, techniques alone can never grow a healthy church. We cannot simply apply methodologies to cure spiritual ailments. The Holy Spirit must be present and active in each development phase. If not, we may end up with principles without power or power without principles, each of which would produce a grotesquely deformed 'body'.

We must remain person not programme oriented. Our trust is not in techniques, but in God, because he alone gives the increase and causes fruitfulness and growth (1 Corinthians 3:5). Our efforts never guarantee fixed results. Growth is God's business. It is a matter of his choosing and our co-operation, in which prayer has an irreplaceable two-way part to play.

After twenty-five years of work in India, the Overseas

Missionary Society could point to only twenty-five churches comprising two thousand believers. Frustrated with that result, they developed and implemented a plan, hopefully to try to see the situation changed.

The plan was simple. They recruited one thousand people in the various homelands from which the overseas missionaries originated, who would be prepared to pray for fifteen minutes daily for their Indian work. Within a few years, explosive growth occurred to where the number of churches reached 550, and the number of believers exceeded seventy-three thousand. [16]

They planned and prayed and obviously God did something he was unable or unwilling to do prior to their prayer plan being implemented.

Endnotes

1. Robert E. Logan, *Beyond Church Growth*. Old Tappan, New Jersey: Fleming H. Revell, 1989, 11–12.

2. *Ibid.*, 18.

3. Peter F. Drucker, Lecture to students at Claremont School of Theology, 30 September, 1971.

4. Edward Dayton and Ted Engstrom, *Strategy for Leadership*. Bromley, Kent: Missions Advance Research Centre, Europe, 1979, 56–58.

5. Ted Engstrom and Edward Dayton, *The Art of Management for Christian Leaders*. Waco, Texas: Word, 1976, 214.

6. Edward Dayton, *Tools for Time Management*. Grand Rapids, Michigan: Zondervan, 1974, 167.

7. Lynn Hirschberg, 'Diana Ross: One Tough Butterfly,' *Good Weekend*, 10 June 1989, 44.

8. Edward Dayton, *Tools for Time Management*, 125.

9. Engstrom and Dayton, *The Art of Management for Christian Leaders*, 45.

10. Ginger Hope, 'Romania's Unchained Melody,' *World Vision*, December 1990–January 1991, 11.

11. Terry Teykl, *Pray and Grow*. Nashville, Tennessee: Discipleship Resources, 1988, 41.

12. Karl Barth, *Prayer and Preaching*. Napperville, Illinois: SCM Book Club, 1964, 21.

13. Terry Muck, *Liberating the Leader's Prayer Life*. Waco, Texas: Word, 1985, 176.

14. Peter Wagner, 'Praying and Growing,' *Ministries Today*, May–June 1990, 56.

15. Peter Wagner, 'The Power of Corporate Prayer.' *Ministries Today*, September–October 1989, 28.

16. George Otis, Jr, *The Last of the Giants*. Tarrytown, New York: Chosen Books, Fleming H. Revell, 1991, 248.

Chapter 8

Go For It

In 1982, Christians in East Germany started to organise small groups of ten to twelve persons committed to meet each Monday night to pray for peace. By October 1989, fifty thousand people were involved in Monday night prayer meetings. [1] In 1990, when those praying moved quietly into the streets, their numbers quickly swelled to 300,000 and the 'wall came tumbling down'.

In Cuba in 1990, an Assemblies of God pastor whose congregation never exceeded one hundred people meeting once per week, suddenly found himself conducting twelve services per day for seven thousand people. They started queuing by 2.00 a.m. and even broke down the doors just to get into the prayer meetings. Asked to explain these phenomena, Cuban Christians say,

> 'It has come because we have paid the price. We have suffered for the Gospel; and we have prayed for many, many years.' [2]

Try as we might, just as in spite of our best efforts we have never been able to explain adequately the mysteries of relationships within the Godhead, we will never be able to understand fully God's ways (Job 11:7–8; Isaiah 55:8–9). All we can deduce is that from the human perspective, if we desire to see God at work growing his church, prayer becomes neither an optional extra nor a position of desperate last resort. It stands as the one indispensable, fundamental factor among all the other needed principles of church growth.

East Africa has been experiencing rapid growth in its cities and some of its churches for some time. Calvary Baptist Church in Mbeya, Tanzania started in 1958 and by 1991 had grown to 600 members. Nairobi Baptist Church in Kenya was also founded in 1958, but in the same period it grew to 2400 regular adult attenders on Sunday mornings. However, Ushindi Baptist Church in Mombasa, Kenya although begun only in 1984, by 1991 already had over 2500 registered members, and over 3000 people in regular Sunday morning attendance. It was also established in the midst of a Muslim community and had no permanent buildings.

Each church has strong, gifted, visionary leadership. Each has good lay training programmes which release members into ministry and especially into new initiatives to meet community needs. Each encourages members to use their spiritual gifts. Each has dynamic worship services, small group or cell ministries, and strong financial support.

However, there is at least one significant difference among these three churches. The largest and most rapidly growing, Ushindi Baptist, has the most dominantly developed prayer ministry, while Calvary Baptist has the least. [3]

Although it can never be proved conclusively, from material presented in this book it may at least be asserted that it is prayer that 'makes all other good church growth principles work'. [4] As we pray, 'Christ's last commandment [becomes] our first concern'. [5]

Today there is great pressure from many directions in society to work harder, to become smarter, to produce results, or be moved aside. The church in many western countries is in danger of absorbing some of this mentality into its own attitudes and work practices, forgetting that in the divine-human endeavour of church growth, 'success' comes not by might, nor by human power, but by a gracious release of God's Holy Spirit (Zechariah 4:6). Any effort we expend on technique, goal setting, planning, or suchlike, can only be little more than setting 'sails in which we hope to catch the wind of the Spirit'.[6]

In the church in the west we have the most up to date state-of-the-art technology available to us to communicate the gospel. However, comparatively little seems to be happening in so many countries in terms of the growth of the church. Could it be that while the world has learned to communicate with robots on Mars, in sections of the church we have forgotten 'to communicate with the Lord of the earth'?[7]

If that is so, and we would desire to see already-discovered church growth principles activated, then perhaps our best course of action is to spend time in the house of the Lord rather than anywhere else (Psalm 84:10–11).

In that the biblical, historical, and contemporary evidence of a strong link between prayer and church growth seems rather conclusive, we need to stand with the company of the first disciples and, like them, return to the Head of the church saying,

'Lord, teach us to pray.'   (Luke 11:1)

Endnotes

1. Evelyn Christenson, United Prayer Ministries Newsletter, Fall 1990, 1.
2. Greg O'Connor, 'Miracles in Cuba,'*New Day, May 1990, 7–9.*
3. James Diedrich, 'Urban Church Growth in East Africa: Three Case Studies,' *Global Church Growth*, January/February/March, 1991, 4–6.
4. Terry Tekyl, *Pray and Grow*. Nashville, Tennessee: Discipleship Resources, 1988, 2.
5. *Ibid.*, 43.
6. Paul Beasley-Murray and Allen Wilkinson, *Turning the Tide*. London: Bible Society, 1981, 87.
7. Selwyn Hughes, *Prayer for Growing Christians*. Surrey, UK: Christian World Review, 1985, 2.

Personal Postscript

After returning from 10 weeks accumulated annual leave which I had used to write the manuscript which has mostly become this book I noticed that my own church had become 'flat'. It seemed to be more or less just going through the motions of church life: Sunday services, committee meetings and activities.

For me, one of the surest indicators of real spiritual productivity has been the presence or absence of conversions. Upon investigation I found that during the period of my absence there had been very few, if any at all. I also discovered that the most significant foundations of our prayer ministry, the daily 6.00 a.m. prayer meetings, had virtually ceased to exist. With the exception of two days per week I was in the prayer room alone. Even the prayer co-ordinator had resigned. Not surprisingly, other problems of a divisive nature had arisen.

What to do was the question.

I resolved that I would not berate, scold or criticise anyone. Neither congregation, staff nor pastoral team needed that sort of knee jerk reaction. I was the Senior Pastor. Before God as shepherd of this flock I was responsible for what had happened and for what would happen.

I resolved to pray and fast until the situation was turned around. Weekly, up in the hills outside of Melbourne and daily at 6.00 a.m. in the prayer room mostly alone, I prayed, fasted, waged warfare and sought the Lord on behalf of the church.

Within three months, supernaturally the Lord spoke to key people to come and join me. Firstly he moved new people into place who would share responsibility for the prayer ministry and then he brought others to join them.

The results?

By the end of three months new leaders and structures had emerged (and I was ten kilograms lighter and almost exhausted!)

By the end of twelve months we saw over one hundred conversions, more than double the total for any single year in the preceding decade.

Appendix 1

References in Acts to Prayer and Church Growth

Prayer reference	Prayer/growth concurrence and kinds of growth
1:14 – ... constantly in prayer	1:15 – ... about 120; numerical
1:24–25 – for Judas' replacement	1:24-25 – organisational
2:42 – devoted ... to prayer	2:47 – added to; numerical
2:47 – praising God daily	4:4 – ... grew to 5,000; numerical
3:1 – at the time of prayer	
4:24–30 – believers' prayer	5:14 – more ... added; numerical
6:4 – ... attention to prayer	6:6 – organisational
6:6 – for deacons	6:7 – increased rapidly; numerical
7:59–60 – of Stephen	8:4–13 – Samaritans believing; numerical
8:15 – Peter and John – for new believers	8:38 – Eunuch baptised; numerical
8:29 – Spirit speaks	
9:5–6 – Saul and the Lord	9:5–6 – Saul believing; numerical
9:10-16 – Ananias and the Lord	9:15–16 – Ananias; commissioning
9:11 – Saul	9:17–20 – Saul; commissioning

Prayer reference	*Prayer/growth concurrence and kinds of growth*
9:40 – for Tabitha	9:42 – many believe; numerical
10:1–7 – of Cornelius 10:9–16 – of Peter	10:48 – Cornelius and company; numerical 11:21 – a great number; numerical
12:5–12 – Peter in prison 13:2–3 – for Barnabas and Saul	13:2–3 – Barnabas and Saul; commissioning
14:23 – appointing elders	14:23 – organisational
15:28 – about advice	15:28 – qualitative 16:5 strengthened ... growing daily; qualitative/numerical
16:6–10 – Macedonian vision	16:6–10 – commissioning
16:13–15 – place of prayer	16:13–15 – Lydia and household; numerical
16:16 – once again ... place of prayer 16:25–34 – in prison	16:33–34 – Philippian jailer's family; numerical 17:4 – large number persuaded; numerical 17:34 – a few believers; numerical 18:7 – Titius and Corinthian believers; numerical
18:9–10 – Paul's vision	18:11 – Paul teaching; qualitative 18:23 – strengthening disciples; qualitative
19:6 – laying on of hands	19:6 – qualitative 19:18 – many believed; numerical 20:2 – speaking encouragement; qualitative

Prayer reference	*Prayer/growth concurrence and kinds of growth*
20:36 – all prayed	10:22–36 – teaching; qualitative
21:4 – Spirit directing	
21:11 – Spirit advising	
22:6–21 – the Lord speaking	22:6–21 – recounting; commissioning
23:11 – the Lord speaking	23:11 – commissioning
26:13–18 – recounting conversion	26:13–18 – commissioning
27:23–24 – Angel speaks	28:15 – encouragement; qualitative
27:35 – giving thanks	
28:8 – for healing	28:24 – some convinced; numerical
28:15 – thanking God	

Appendix 2

Prayer Co-ordinator's Job Description

Position Title

Prayer Co-ordinator

The Person

The co-ordinator will be a mature church member who, by example and experience, will have demonstrated a long-term interest in and practice of prayer.

The person should preferably have a vision for this ministry and be prepared to develop it further. The appointee will be a good team person, able to lead, motivate, and encourage others in leadership of this ministry department.

The person will need a proven ability to keep confidences and will have demonstrable sensitivity skills in interpersonal relationships. Basic typing/word processing skills and some experience in administration are desirable but not essential. Upon appointment, the person would need to relinquish all other responsibilities in the church to major on this calling.

Accountability

The co-ordinator will be accountable to the senior pastor with whom the appointee will meet monthly to review ministry, progress, and needs.

Key Activities

1. To recruit and retain a group of people who share a vision for prayer and who will assist the co-ordinator.
2. To liaise with all other departmental prayer leaders of the church.
3. To be responsible for the publication and distribution of all prayer materials in all media throughout the church.
4. To keep up to date records of all prayer activity across the church.
5. To spend time personally in prayer and fasting seeking the Holy Spirit's future direction for the development of the ministry.

Conditions

The initial appointment is for a period of twelve months and is renewable annually subject to mutual agreement between the appointee and the senior pastor.

Remuneration

Financial – nil.
Spiritual – unlimited, beyond imagining (Ephesians 3:20).

Appendix 3

Prayer Department Organisational Chart

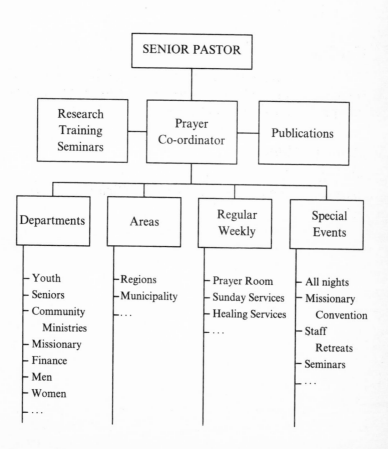

SENIOR PASTOR

Research Training Seminars

Prayer Co-ordinator

Publications

Departments
- Youth
- Seniors
- Community Ministries
- Missionary
- Finance
- Men
- Women
- . . .

Areas
- Regions
- Municipality
- . . .

Regular Weekly
- Prayer Room
- Sunday Services
- Healing Services
- . . .

Special Events
- All nights
- Missionary Convention
- Staff Retreats
- Seminars
- . . .

Selected Bibliography

Arndt, W.F., and Gingrich, F.W. *A Greek English Lexicon*. Chicago: University of Chicago Press, 1957.

Bagster, Samuel. *The Analytical Greek Lexicon*. London: Samuel Bagster and Sons, 1967.

Barth, Karl. *Prayer and Preaching*. Napperville, Illinois: SCM Book Club, 1964.

Beasley-Murray, Paul and Wilkinson, Alan. *Turning the Tide*. London: Bible Society, 1981.

Billheimer, Paul E. *Destined for the Throne*. Fort Washington, Pennsylvania: Christian Literature Crusade, 1975.

Blaiklock, E.M. *Acts*. London: Tyndale, 1959.

Bounds, E.M. *Prayer and Praying Men*. Grand Rapids, Michigan: Baker Book House, 1977.

Bright, Vonette and Jennings, Ben A. *Unleashing the Power of Prayer*. Chicago: Moody Press, 1989.

Broomhall, Marshall. *The Jubilee Story of the China Inland Mission*. London: Morgan and Scott Ltd, 1915.

Bryant, David. *Concerts of Prayer*. Ventura, California: Regal Books, 1984.

Bryant, David. *Prayer Pacesetters Sourcebook*. Minneapolis, Minnesota: Concerts of Prayer International, 1989.

Chaney, Charles L., and Lewis, Ron S. *Design for Church Growth*. Nashville, Tennessee: Broadman, 1977.

Cho, Paul Y. *Prayer: Key to Revival*. Waco, Texas: Word Books, 1984.

Cho, Paul Y., and Manzano, R. Whitney. *More Than Numbers*. Gwent, UK: Valley Books, 1983.

Christenson, Evelyn. *What Happens When Women Pray*. Wheaton, Illinois: Victor Books, 1975.

Crossman, Eileen. *Mountain Rain*. Singapore: Overseas Missionary Fellowship, 1982.

Dallmore, A. *C.H. Spurgeon*. Chicago: Moody Press, 1984.

Dawson, John. *Taking our Cities for God*. Milton Keynes, England: Word Books, 1989.

Dayton, Edward and Engstrom, Ted. *Strategy for Leadership*. Bromley, Kent: Missions Advanced Research Centre, Europe, 1979.

Dinsdale T. and Young, C.H. *Spurgeon's Prayers*. New York: Revell, 1906.

Duewel, Wesley L. *Touch the World Through Prayer*. Grand Rapids, Michigan: Francis Ashbury Press, 1986.

Eastman, Dick. *The Hour that Changes the World*. Grand Rapids, Michigan: Baker Book House, 1978.

Eastman, Dick. *Change the World School of Prayer*. Penshurst, Australia: World Literature Crusade, 1983.

Ellul, Jaques. *Prayer and Modern Man*. New York: Seabury Press, 1970.

Engstrom, Ted and Dayton, Edward. *The Art of Management for Christian Leaders*. Waco, Texas: Word Books, 1976.

Frangipane, Francis. *The House of the Lord*. Milton Keynes, England: Word Publishing, 1992.

Fraser, O.J. and Taylor, Mrs Howard. *Fraser and Prayer*. London: China Inland Mission, 1963.

Garrison, David V. *The Nonresidential Missionary*. New Hope, Alabama: Missions Advanced Research Centre, 1990.

Gibbs, Eddie. *I Believe in Church Growth*. London: Hodder and Stoughton, 1981.

Goforth, Rosalind. *Jonothan Goforth*. Minneapolis, Minnesota: Bethany House, 1986.

Grubb, Norman. *Rees Howells Intercessor*. London: Lutterworth Press, 1952.

Hallesby, O. *Prayer*. London: Inter-Varsity Press, 1965.

Hesselgrave, J. *Planting Churches Cross-Culturally*. Grand Rapids, Michigan: Baker Book House, 1978.

Hodges, Melvin L. *A Guide to Church Planting*. Chicago: Moody Press, 1973.

Hollenweger, Walter J. *The Pentecostals*. Minneapolis, Minnesota: Augsburg, 1972.

Hughes, Selwyn. *Prayer for Growing Christians*. Surrey, UK: Christian World Revival, 1985.

Hunter, Bingham. *The God Who Hears*. Downers Grove, Illinois: Inter-Varsity Press, 1986.

Jay, Eric G. *New Testament Greek*. London: SPCK, 1961.

Jensen, Ron and Stevens, Jim. *Dynamics of Church Growth*. Grand Rapids, Michigan: Baker Book House, 1981.

Kane, J. Herbert. *The Christian Mission Today and Tomorrow*. Grand Rapids, Michigan: Baker Book House, 1981.

Klimionok, Reginald. *Levels of Church Growth*. Slacks Creek, Queensland: Assembly Press, 1984.

Latourette, Kenneth Scott. *A History of the Expansion of Christianity*. Vol. VI, *The Great Century in Northern Africa and Asia (AD 1880–1914)*. London: Eyre and Spottiswoode. 1944.

Lea, Larry. *Could You Not Tarry One Hour?* Altamonte Springs, Florida: Creation House, 1987.

Lea, Larry. *Praying With Jesus*. Altamonte Springs, Florida: Creation House, 1987.

Lea, Larry. *The Hearing Ear*. Altamonte Springs, Florida: Creation House, 1988.

Lebsack, Lee. *10 at the Top: How 10 of America's Largest Assemblies of God Churches Grew*. Stowe, Ohio: New Hope Press, 1974.

Linthicum, Robert C. *City of God City of Satan*. Grand Rapids, Michigan: Zondervan, 1991.

Lloyd-Jones, Martyn. *Revival*. Westchester, Illinois: Crossway Books, 1987.

Logan, Robert E. *Beyond Church Growth*. Old Tappan, New Jersey: Fleming H. Revell, 1989.

McClung, Floyd. *Spirits of the City*. Sussex, UK: Kingsway, 1990.

McGavran, Donald. *Understanding Church Growth*. Bombay: Eerdmans, 1970.

Mills, Brian. *Three Plus Three Equals Twelve*. Eastbourne: Kingsway Publications, 1986.

Muck, Terry. *Liberating the Leader's Prayer Life*. Waco, Texas: Word Books, 1985.

Orr, J. Edwin. *The Second Evangelical Awakening*. London: Marshall, Morgan and Scott, 1955.

Orr, J. Edwin. *The Flaming Tongue. The Impact of 20th Century Revivals*. Chicago: Moody Press, 1973.

Orr, J. Edwin. *The Fervent Prayer. The World Wide Impact of the Great Awakening of 1858*. Chicago: Moody Press, 1974.

Orr, J. Edwin. *The Eager Feet. Evangelical Awakenings 1790–1830*. Chicago: Moody Press, 1975.

Otis, George, Jr. *The Last of the Giants*. Tarrytown, New York: Chosen Books, Fleming H. Revell, 1991.

Penn-Lewis, Jessie. *Prayer and Evangelism*. Dorset, England: Overcomer Publications, n.d.

Peters, George. W. *Evangelical Missions Tomorrow*. Pasadena, California: William Carey Library Publications, 1977.

Peters, George. W. *A Theology of Church Growth*. Grand Rapids, Michigan: Zondervan, 1981.

Prince, Derek. *Shaping History Through Prayer and Fasting*. Fort Lauderdale, Florida: Derek Prince Ministries, 1973.

Rinker, Rosalind. *Prayer. Conversing With God*. Grand Rapids, Michigan: Zondervan, 1959.

Shibley, David. *Let's Pray in the Harvest*. Rockwall, Texas: Church on the Rock, 1985.

Smail, Tom. *The Forgotten Father*. London: Hodder and Stoughton, 1980.

Taylor, Mrs Howard. *Behind the Ranges Fraser of Lisuland South West China*. London: OMF 1944.

Teykl, Terry. *Pray and Grow*. Nashville, Tennessee: Discipleship Resources, 1988.

Torrey, R.A. *The Power of Prayer*. Grand Rapids, Michigan: Zondervan, 1974.

Towns, Elmer L., Vaughan, John N. and Serfert, David J. *The Complete Book of Church Growth*. Wheaton, Tyndale: 1981.

Virkler, Mark. *Dialogue with God*. Woy Woy, NSW: Peacemakers, 1987.

Wagner, C. Peter. *Leading Your Church to Growth*. Ventura, California: Regal Books, 1984.

Wagner, C. Peter. *Your Church Can Grow*. Ventura, California: Regal Books, 1984.

Wagner, C. Peter. *Wrestling with Dark Angels*. Eastbourne, England: Monarch Publications, 1990.

Wagner, C. Peter. *Warfare Prayer*. Tunbridge Wells, UK: Monarch Publications, 1992.

Wagner, C. Peter. *Prayer Shield*. Ventura, California: Regal Books, 1992.

Wang, David. *And They Continued Steadfastly*. Hong Kong: Asian Outreach International Ltd, n.d.

Wang, David. *Eight Lessons We Can Learn From the Church in China*. Hong Kong: Asian Outreach International Ltd, n.d.

When People Pray. Singapore: Overseas Missionary Fellowship, 1987.

Willhite, Bob J. *Why Pray?* Altamonte Springs, Florida: Creation House, 1988.

Articles

Australian Fellowship of Church Growth 4 (April 1990).

Barton, David. 'Did School Prayer Work?' *Ministries Today*, May/June 1991, 97.

Buckley, Mark. 'Lessons From Desert Storm.' *Ministries Today*, May/June 1991, 110.

Cedar, Paul. 'A Pastor's Perspective of Building a Praying Church.' In *Unleashing the Power of Prayer*, ed. Vonette Bright and Ben A. Jennings, 193–200. Chicago: Moody Press, 1989.

'Cross Over Australia. Baptists Together in Evangelism.' Spring 1987, 4–5.

Cunningham, Loren. 'The Caleb Report.' *Ministries Today*, January/February 1990, 62.

Davies, Evan. 'Where Have All the Prayer Meetings Gone?' *New Life*, October 1989, 6.

Diedrich, James. 'Urban Church Growth in East Africa: Three Case Studies.' *Global Church Growth*, January/February/March 1991, 4–6.

Douglas, Merril E. and McNally, J. 'How Ministers Use Their Time.' *The Christian Ministry*, January 1980, 23.

Drayton, Dean. 'Life or Death.' *On Being*, June 1986, 7.

Dudley, Roger L. and Cummings, Des. 'A Study of Factors Relating to Church Growth in the North American Division of Seventh Day Adventists.' *Review of Religious Research*, 24 (June 1983): 322–33.

Edgerly, George. 'Survey of Pastors of 1974's Fastest Growing Schools.' Springfield, Missouri: Assemblies of God, n.d.

Graham, Duncan. 'He Shall Not Be Moved.' *Good Weekend*, 16 November 1991, 68.

Hay, Ian M. 'Uplifted Hands.' *SIM Now*, July/August 1990, 8.

Hirschberg, Lynn. 'Diana Ross: One Tough Butterfly.' *Good Weekend*, 10 June 1989, 44.

Hope, Ginger. 'Romania's Unchained Melody.' *World Vision*, December 1990/January 1991, 11.

Iyer, Pico. 'The Art of Life.' *Time*, 18 December 1989, 74, 77.

Kuzmic, Peter. 'Pentecostal Fervour in Eastern Europe.'
World Missions Update, October 1991, 3–4.

Lambert, Tony. 'Return to Tiananmen – One Year After.'
The Queensland Baptist, August 1990, 8.

Lambert, Tony. 'China Crisis.' *Alpha*, August 1991, 20.

Lindsell, Harold. 'Prayer and the Battle for the World.' In
Unleashing the Power of Prayer, ed. Vonette Bright
and Ben A. Jennings, 294–296. Chicago: Moody Press,
1989.

Lovelace, Richard. 'What Can We Learn From Past
Spiritual Awakenings?' In *Unleashing the Power of
Prayer*, ed. Vonette Bright and Ben A.

Jennings, 139–152. Chicago: Moody Press, 1989.

Kantzer, Kenneth S. 'What Happens When Christians
Pray.' *Christianity Today*, August 1993, 13.

Marocco, James. 'Prayer Therapy.' *Church Growth*, June
1989, 16.

McIntosh, Duncan. 'Prayer is the Key to Church Growth.'
The Victorian Baptist Witness, August 1990, 4.

Muck, Terry. 'Ten Questions About the Devotional Life.'
Leadership, Winter 1982, 34.

Nicholls, A.G. 'How God is Working Among the Tribes.'
China's Millions, January 1919, 4.

O'Connor, Greg. 'Miracles in Cuba.' *New Day*, May 1990,
7–9.

'Palm Beach Proves Power of Prayer.' *The Queensland
Baptist*, November 1989, 7.

Piggin, Stuart. 'Revivals Common in Australia.' *The
Victorian Baptist Witness*, August 1991, 17.

'Prayer Triplets Bring Joy.' *National Baptist*, December
1988, 15.

Sheppard, Glen. 'Prayer for Spiritual Awakening.'
Decision, March 1988, 12.

Silvoso, Edgardo. 'The Principle Behind the Strategy.'
Harvest Now, September/October 1990, 4.

Spicer, Charles W. Jr. 'It's True! High Estimates of
Christian Converts in China Confirmed.' *Overseas
Council Newsletter*, n.d., 3.

Wagner, C. Peter. 'The Power of Corporate Prayer.'
   Ministries Today, September/October 1989, 28.
Wagner, C. Peter. 'Praying for Leaders.' *Equipping the
   Saints*, Spring 1990, 23-27.
Wagner, C. Peter. 'Praying and Growing.' *Ministires
   Today*, May/June 1990, 56.
Wagner, C. Peter. 'Argentina's Annacondia.' *Ministries
   Today*, September/October 1990, 36.
Wagner, C. Peter. 'Spiritual Power in Urban Evangelism:
   Dynamic Lessons from Argentina.' *Evangelical
   Missions Quarterly*, 27 (April 1991): 132.
Wagner, C. Peter. '1990: The Hinge Between Past and
   Future.' *Ministries Today*, May/June 1991, 32.
Wagner, C. Peter. 'Hunting in the Heavenlies.' *On Being*,
   July 1991, 7.
Wang, David. 'And They Continued Steadfastly – Part I.'
   Asian Report, July/August 1993, 22.
Wang, David. 'And They Continued Steadfastly – Part II.'
   Asian Report, September/October 1993, 20–23.
Wiggin, Eric E. 'The Church Since Chairman Mao.'
   Moody Monthly, October 1988, 85.
Willhite, B.J. 'How to Get Your People to Pray.'
   Ministries Today, November/December 1988, 32–37.
Williams, Jim. 'Seoul Secrets.' *Church Growth*, June 1989,
   8.
'Worthwhile and Exciting.' *National Baptist*, September
   1988, 14.

Bible References
All Bible references unless otherwise stated are: New
   International Version. Grand Rapids, Michigan:
   Zondervan, 1978.

Manuals
Church Growth II lectures, Pasadena, August 1988.

Primary Sources

Arndell, R. Seaton. 'Revival in the Enga Church,' TMs, 1973. Original in the hand of the author, Sydney.

Arndell, R. Seaton. 'The Revival Among the Kyaka Enga People of Papua New Guinea,' TMs, n.d. Original in the hand of the author, Sydney.

Clinton, Bob. 'Fasting, Prayer and Church Growth,' TMs, n.d. Original in the hand of the author, Melbourne.

Denton, Rodney. 'Asian Trip August 18-September 7,' TMs, September 1985. Blackburn Baptist Church Archives, Melbourne.

Denton, Rodney. 'Argentina, The Land of the Awakened Church.' Unpublished MA research paper, Fuller Theological Seminary, Pasadena, 1991.

Lambert, Tony. 'Patterns of Growth and Continuity: The Historical Context.' Uncompleted MPhil diss., 1991.

Van Houton, Richard. 'The State of the Church in China,' TMs, 1984. Original in the hand of author, Hong Kong, 5.

If you have enjoyed this book and would like to help us to send a copy of it and many other titles to needy pastors in the **Third World**, please write for further information or send your gift to:

Sovereign World Trust
PO Box 777, Tonbridge
Kent TN11 0ZS
United Kingdom

or to the **'Sovereign World'** distributor in your country.